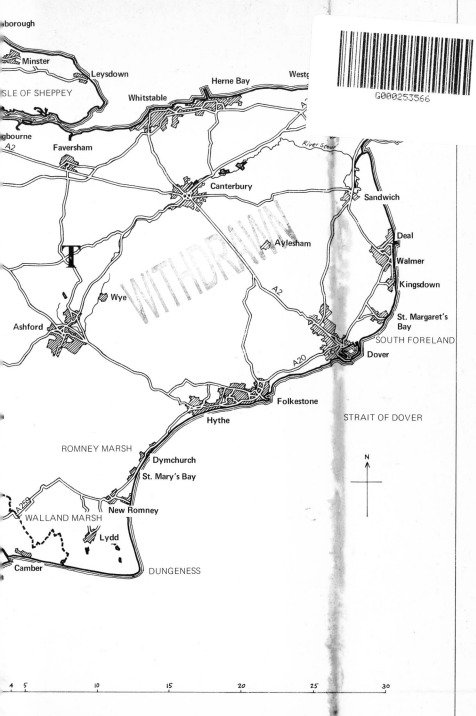

borough

Minster   Leysdown

ISLE OF SHEPPEY   Whitstable   Herne Bay   Westg

gbourne   Faversham   River Stour
A2

Canterbury   Sandwich

T   WITHDRAWN   Aylesham   Deal

Walmer

Wye   A2   Kingsdown

Ashford   St. Margaret's
Bay
A20   SOUTH FORELAND
Dover

Folkestone   STRAIT OF DOVER

Hythe

ROMNEY MARSH   N

Dymchurch

St. Mary's Bay

A259   New Romney
WALLAND MARSH

Lydd

Camber   DUNGENESS

4 5   10   15   20   25   30

P SHOWING THE CINQUE PORTS

F ·ry, People and Places

of

·UE PORTS

Arms of the Cinque Ports. Rye Town Hall [*Photo J. Wood*]

History, People and Places

of

THE CINQUE PORTS

EDWARD HININGS

SPURBOOKS LIMITED

Published By
Spurbooks Ltd
6 Parade Court
Bourne End
Buckinghamshire

© Edward Hinings 1975

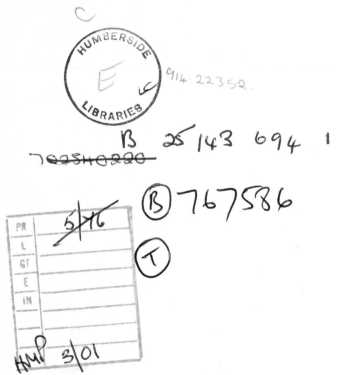

ISBN 0 902875 90 6

MADE AND PRINTED IN GREAT BRITAIN BY
THE GARDEN CITY PRESS LIMITED
LETCHWORTH, HERTFORDSHIRE SG6 IJS

Contents

Illustrations

Acknowledgements

In writing even a brief history on a subject as complex as that of the Cinque Ports an author is faced with an immense amount of work in researching the mass of material available to him. If he is as fortunate as I have been, his task is made very much easier by the generous help and advice of others, to whom he can only offer sincere and grateful thanks.

In particular, I wish to thank Dr. Felix Hull, Kent County archivist for his unfailing courtesy and readiness to help. Also Miss Anne Roper, of Littlestone, for all the trouble she took to answer my numerous queries and for using her good offices to make it possible for me to attend the historic sitting of the Court of Brotherhood and Guestling at Hythe on October 12th last year.

My thanks also to Mr. Harry Margary for permission to reproduce photographs of Lympne Castle: to Mr. J. D. Smith, Town Clerk of Rye and to the Rye Council for allowing me to use the pictures by Mr. J. Wood, of the Cinque Ports Arms and the insignia of Rye: to Lord Astor of Hever for his help in tracing the appointment as Lord Warden of Anne Boleyn's brother, Lord Rochfort. Also I wish to thank the Manchester University Press for permission to photograph and use their map of the Cinque Ports from the frontispiece of K. M. E. Murray's Constitutional History of the Cinque Ports: Mr. Edward Reeves of Lewes for the photographs of the Winchelsea Seal, and the Town Clerk of Sandwich for his help in

9

tracing some of the unique customs and traditions of that ancient port.

Finally, to my family and friends who have borne with me while this work was in progress, and to Peter Walker of Crowborough who resolved a crisis with the loan of his typewriter—my deepest gratitude!

Edward Hinings
Sussex, 1975

CHAPTER I

Origin of the Ports

In a letter to the Speaker of the Court of Brotherhood and Guestling of the Cinque Ports, Mark Antony Lower, a Freeman of Seaford wrote—

'I cannot but deeply regret that circumstances I cannot control prevent my accepting your very kind invitation to be present at your deliberations upon the state and affairs of the Cinque Ports. I assure you that I feel deeply indebted for your politeness in requesting my attendance upon so honourable and interesting an occasion.

'For every Englishman who values the Wooden Walls of our beloved country, for every patriot who regards with pride the growth and development of our free institutions, the Cinque Ports should possess a charm of no ordinary character. Their antiquity transcends historical research but there can be little doubt they arose out of the Municipal regulations of Roman times at an early period of civilisation in this island.

In later days the Fleet of the Cinque Ports was at once the glory and defence of our land, as it was the first germ of that naval supremacy which has made the English flag an object of respect and veneration throughout the world.

From St. Anne's House in Lewes that 28th day of October 1857,

Mark Antony Lower.

Mark Antony Lower's reference to Roman times was no doubt inspired by the chain of fortresses built by the Romans in the third century and which extended along the coastline from Cromer to the Isle of Wight. They were known as the Saxon-Shore forts and the commander-in-chief of the forces deployed there enjoyed the romantic title of Count of the Saxon Shore.

There were nine of these forts in all, of which the more important were Reculver, Dover and Pevensey. When the Conqueror landed near Pevensey in 1066 he evidently appreciated the strategic value of the great fort, built as it was on a promontory which provided a safe landfall for the patrolling Roman fleet. The massive outer walls, with their fifteen rounded bastions, of which ten remain, enclosed approximately ten acres. The Conqueror's half brother, Robert of Mortain, was given the lordship of Pevensey and proceeded to build his Norman castle inside the Roman walls which provided him with an almost impregnable curtain wall that made the castle secure against anything in the nature of a surprise attack.

The history of the Confederation we know as the Cinque Ports goes back to the reign of Edward the Confessor. Eadbright in 732 is credited by some historians with having attempted to establish something of the kind, but whatever he achieved could only have been restricted by the conflicting claims of the petty kingdoms into which Southern England was then divided. Nevertheless, having regard to the main reason for the existence of the Saxon shore forts the idea is attractive.

The fact that such a confederation could exist is of more than casual interest. Such a confederation would be in almost violent contrast to the accepted order of things at the time, so that its origins assume an importance out of all keeping with its aims and objects. Controversy has waxed fierce over the whole question of pre- or post-Conquest origin, one of the main supporters of the former theory being Montague Burrows. J. H. Round dismisses his ideas, however, substituting one based upon the evidence of the customs of the Ports concerned. This does not necessarily mean there was no official association of the ports before the Charter of Edward I. According to Miss Murray, in her *Constitutional History of the Cinque Ports* there is evidence of the Ports acting in concert during the reign of King John. Arguments in favour of this theory are largely based upon the simultaneous grant by John in 1205 of a series of charters to each of the five ports and to Rye and Winchelsea. Those to Rye and Winchelsea have the added interest of confirming an earlier one of Richard I.

What both Round and Burrows appear to overlook or ignore is that the Cinque Ports Confederation was the outcome of specialised local conditions, just as the Roman forts were. The same pressures were brought to bear on the ports as upon the Romans due to the fact that they were sited on a coastline constantly under attack and commanding a seaway which cut across the maritime highway linking England with the Continent.

The original composition of the Confederation consisted of the five Head Ports. These were Hastings, Romney, Hythe, Dover and Sandwich. To these were added Winchelsea and Rye, the two 'antient towns'. These ports were linked together in an association with common duties to perform, in return for which they were granted special privileges. The most important of the obligations imposed upon them was the provision of fifty-seven ships, fully manned, for fifteen days service a year, each port being allocated a share of the total burden.

This service was the essence of the confederation. Nevertheless, the importance of the part played by the ports in respect of ship-service, has been considerably over-emphasised, for at no time in their long history were the ports the sole source of ships for the Navy.

On the other hand the possession of bases on the south-eastern seaboard gave the Portsmen absolute control of a

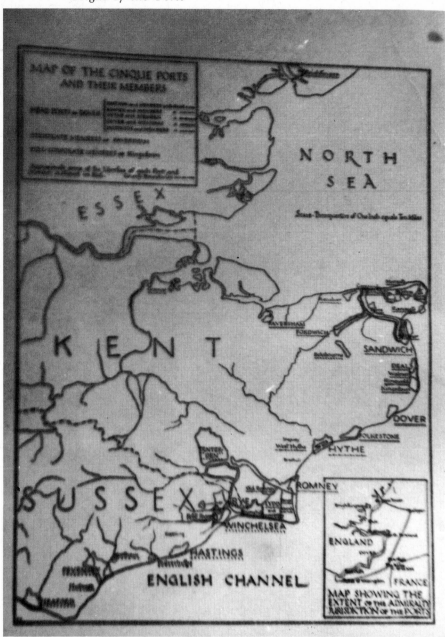

Map showing original Admiralty jurisdiction of the Cinque Ports

vital section of the English Channel. Without the consent of the Ports no one could cross to the Continent and in time of civil war the different sides would make strenuous efforts to come to terms with the members of the Confederation. The opportunities thus afforded for blackmail were both numerous and tempting and in a period beset by civil wars the uncertain loyalties of the Ports was one of the chief factors in producing the charters granted in 1205.

In these, one of the chief of the many privileges granted was freedom from customary taxation such as *lastage* (duty by weight), *tallage* (duty by number), *passage* (tax on landing), *rivage*, (wharf toll), and *infangtheff* (the right to judge thieves taken within the precincts of the Ports).

In return, as already pointed out, the Ports undertook to furnish fifty-seven ships for fifteen days each year. We could be excused from thinking that the King would claim the right of ship service for as long as might be necessary, but if we accept that, on the available evidence, Edward the Confessor originated the confederation, it becomes easier to understand why an arbitrary term of fifteen days was fixed. This was, presumably, based on two factors. One, the Danish raids at that time took place generally once a year and were quickly over, and fifteen days was the time allowed for a voyage to the Continent and back.

The 13th century saw the Ports becoming ever more important. This fact is underlined by the extension of the liberties of the original confederation to include the admission of 'Limbs' or 'Members'. By the association of places as far apart as Chatham in Kent and Pevensey in Sussex, the entire coast line with its smallest creeks and harbours came under the direct control of the Portsmen. It was then that, for the first time, something in the nature of an official list was compiled, giving the names of the head ports, their members and the quota of ships assigned to each. Hastings had ten members, Romney five, Hythe one, Dover three and Sandwich five. Later changes recorded the inclusion of a group of parishes in Thanet, and Seaford was incorporated a member of Hastings in 1544. In the 14th century Reculver dropped out, having been virtually swept away by the sea. Rye and Winchelsea were later elevated to the status of Head Ports, their combined service having been advanced from two to fifteen ships.

All the evidence of the early charters clearly implies that the Ports were considered as a unit and the existence of a common court at Shepway confirms this. The Shepway was the earliest of the courts common to the confederation, its constitution plainly revealing the influences which contributed to its powers. These were the King's interests, the jealously guarded liberties of the Ports, and the authority of the Lord Warden, whose appointment was upheld by the court.

One of the cornerstones of the structure thus created was the common interest of the Portsmen in the annual herring fair held at Yarmouth. This alone would seem to supply the economic motive for the confederation which might otherwise seem lacking. In her book, Miss Murray points out that it gave the association a local interest which the performance of a common duty could never have provided by itself.

Implicit with this was the right of 'den' and 'strond' claimed by the Portsmen, a right bitterly resented by the Norfolk fishermen. It was a right which empowered the Portsmen to land without fee and to sell their fish and dry their nets on the strand. The Portsmen practically took over the Herring Fair as well, sending bailiffs to Yarmouth to assume control. So bitter was the enmity between the two factions that it would be no exaggeration to say that something akin to civil war grew out of it, frequently erupting into violence. Fighting took place nearly every time the rivals happened to meet and every method of harassment was employed, from demanding unjust customs to robbery and murder. Matthew Paris records that in 1254, in the reign of Henry III, when the Queen was going from Winchelsea to the Continent, the Yarmouth fishermen sent a large ship with a crew of thirty to carry Prince Edward. The incensed Portsmen of Winchelsea attacked the Yarmouth ship, killing some of the crew and, taking the mast out of the destroyed vessel fitted it to the one intended for the Queen.

There were numerous similar incidents before the turn of the century, one of the worst occurred in 1297 when Edward I was assembling a fleet to attack the French. Fighting broke out between the Cinque Ports contingent and the Yarmouth ships, resulting in twenty-nine of the latter being destroyed and over two hundred men killed. Losses in ships and material were estimated at over £5,000.

The Herring Fair was, however, much too important to be allowed to lapse merely because the two factions were carrying on a war of attrition. The royal awards of 1277 and 1305 incorporated in their respective charters were an attempt to establish peace but merely united the Portsmen in their opposition to any kind of legislation which they considered threatened their liberties. Fighting flared up from time to time and admirals learned that it was very wise to keep the rival factions apart when they met at sea!

Nothing, in fact, that the King or his advisers could do ended a feud which lasted until the 17th century when the Ports finally and voluntarily surrendered their rights.

The Courts of Shepway, Brodhull and Guestling, were the offspring of a growing need to control the affairs of the Ports, to smooth over the fierce rivalries between the Ports themselves and to administer justice. The Court of Shepway, which had the blessing of royal recognition, became the means by which the King could exercise some form of control over his turbulent subjects. The Courts of Brodhull and Guestling, later combined into the Courts of Brotherhood and Guestling, were established by the Portsmen themselves and were set up primarily to protect their privileges and to oversee the regulation of the annual Herring Fair.

As we have seen, the friction between the Norfolk fishermen and the Portsmen was such that the royal awards made in 1277, 1305 and 1357 did little to alleviate the situation. For it was under these awards that the Ports became entitled to send Bailiffs to the Herring Fair, ostensibly to administer justice in co-operation with the Bailiffs of Yarmouth! The election of these bailiffs was the business of the Courts of Brodhull and Guestling. Until the end of the 14th century individual ports elected their own bailiffs to represent them at Yarmouth, but from 1360 the practice of sending only four bailiffs was established. Ports were arranged in groups as, for example, Rye, Winchelsea and Hastings and each group provided one representative.

The composition of these Courts was pseudo Parliamentary. Sittings were, and still are, presided over by a Speaker and members enjoyed immunity from arrest similar to that enjoyed by members of Parliament, and though the Courts were at one time granted special powers, they spoke with one voice for the Ports in a way no other representative body could have done.

Very little is known of the early history of the Court of Shepway. From its first mention in the charter of Henry II and further evidence contained in other charters of similar date, it would be safe to assume that the right of the Portsmen to a court of pleas had long been established. Miss Murray points out that the Constitution and functions of the Court attest to its early origin, prior to the appointment of the Constable of Dover Castle as Lord Warden.

The Court met at irregular intervals but could be called together by the Lord Warden, writs being sent to the Head Ports and Corporate members at least forty days before the appointed date of assembly. The Court would be composed of officers of the various Ports together with

The Shepway Cross, Lympne

townsmen elected for the purpose. From these a jury of twelve would be empanelled, selected by the Warden and each would be sworn to 'enquire and speak the truth of all articles and to receive what is enjoined on the part of the King'. In those days Freemen of the Ports were called barons, but later only those attending a Coronation were so described.

The proceedings were in English and were recorded by a clerk duly appointed for the purpose. From the records which have survived it becomes clear that the Court was concerned mainly with the King's interests. Among the disputes heard were those with Yarmouth, claims by other towns against the Portsmen and—as in 1243—claims about goods plundered from Flemish merchants. If this sounds strange, it should be remembered that from the 13th to the 16th century the fiercest and most rapacious pirates of the time were often men of the Cinque Ports, a great many of their piratical enterprises being so continuous that they could be regarded as private wars. In passing judgement, however, it should be taken into account that piracy was a recognised and legitimate part of naval warfare and that some of the most prominent families took part in, and profited from, activities of this kind. In 1242, for example, the Cinque Ports fleet was instructed by the King to harry the French coast, and it is said that he took a substantial share of the profits.

Records of other, less creditable stories of the Portsmen's forays have come down to us, such as when they attacked the Jews who had been expelled in 1290, and after robbing them of their money, killed great numbers and threw their bodies into the sea. Vested in the court was the power to pass judgement in cases of felony, for crimes such as treason and murder and for numerous lesser offences. For treason and murder the sentence was nearly always death, sentence being carried out immediately. Less serious crimes were punished by fines or imprisonment.

Court of Brotherhood and Guestling. Hythe, October 1973. Address
to the Speaker

It was not, of course, always possible for those summoned to a Court to be present when ordered. As the barons of the Courts were mainly seafaring men the business of the Court had to be adjusted to suit the circumstances. At various times members would be absent at sea, where storms or contrary winds could delay their return for weeks and even months. In this the King's interest was also involved, for it would have been inexpedient and, at times, disastrous to have some enterprise delayed or cancelled because those taking part had been summoned to attend a sitting of the Court. In fact, the town Courts were always suspended during the herring fishing season.

It was the duty of the Lord Warden to maintain and defend the liberties of the Ports, and the Court of Shepway was perhaps the most powerful instrument in discharging this duty. The Portsmen had a vested interest in supporting the Court which otherwise would have been merely a symbol. Nevertheless neither the Lord Warden nor the Portsmen themselves were powerful enough to win a complete immunity from outside interference, although they came very close to doing so.

The history of the Court of Shepway is very largely the history of the Confederation. At first merely a local Court, developed to meet the special needs of the Ports, it became the sole external Court recognised by them, for at this time their liberties were such as to render them virtually immune from the authority of the King's judges.

The special position of the Lord Warden made all this possible. His office rapidly became one of permanent authority over the Ports and as the King's representative he was the link between the royal interests and the Portsmen. In a sense, therefore, he served two masters, for although he received his commission from the King, on taking office he had to swear to uphold the liberties of the Ports come what may, and against all folk.

Before this, the administration of the Confederation was divided between the Bailiffs and the Constable of Dover. In this there were obvious disadvantages. In a civil war, for example, such as that which led to Simon de Montfort's defeat of Henry III at Lewes, the control of the Channel became an issue of paramount importance. There was an obvious danger in having a divided command, for without the strong military base afforded by Dover, the Warden's position would be gravely weakened while still leaving him responsible for the other ports. The obvious solution was to combine the two offices, and this was done.

There were other reasons why such a move was necessary. Apart from the strategic necessity of a unified command the lawless independence of the Ports was a state of affairs which could not be allowed to continue, with the result that from the time of Stephen de Pencestre (1268–1298) the two offices were never again separated.

With the amalgamation, the Wardenship became enhanced, for it became accepted that the bestowal of the title was the mark of the King's favour. Among those who held office from time to time we find the Duke of York and, in the 15th century, the Prince of Wales, the Earl of Arundel and the Duke of Gloucester. During the reign of Henry VIII, Anne Boleyn's brother, Lord Rochfort was amongst those appointed Warden and during Elizabeth's reign the Earl of Essex contested for the prize but was defeated by Lord Cobham.

The office of Lord Warden still survives but its character has changed. It no longer carries with it the prestige and authority vested in the 'Judge Supreme of the Court of Shepway' but is merely an honour bestowed on men whose long and faithful service to the Crown is thus recognised. Lords Warden of the 19th and 20th centuries include William Pitt, the Duke of Wellington (who died in Walmer Castle, Sir Winston Churchill, and Sir Robert Menzies.

CHAPTER II

The Courts of Brodhull and Guestling

As already stated, the Courts were established to safe-guard the liberties of the Ports and were later combined into the Court of Brotherhood and Guestling. The business of the courts was varied, from the appointment of Bailiffs to Yarmouth, to the settling of disputes between the Portsmen themselves. It was the business of the Court of Shepway to swear in a new Lord Warden and to make arrangements for the attendance of the Barons at a Coronation.

The Guestling, so named from the place of its inception, began as a meeting of the ports of Hastings, Rye and Winchelsea. For a time it remained an occasional exped-ient but the constant vigilance required to uphold and maintain privileges created a need for more frequent meetings, so that gradually the Court assumed an import-ance that broke new ground and made it an integral part of the system.

The Brotherhood had largely grown out of the need to provide the service which was responsible for sending bailiffs to Yarmouth and to deal with their reports and accounts. The decreasing importance of the Yarmouth service brought about the inevitable decline in the im-portance of the Brotherhood. At a meeting held at New Romney on July 24th 1655, the matter was referred to the Committee for Grievances and in 1663 the Yarmouth service was suspended for ever.

Court of Brotherhood and Guestling. Hythe, October 1973. Procession
leaving Church

We are fortunate in having the minutes of the meetings of the Brotherhood and Guestling from the 15th century to the present day, for without these much of the history of the Ports would have been lost. These were stored at New Romney where the meetings of the Ports were usually held, and are now available in book form as The Black and White Books of the Cinque Ports. Edited and arranged by Dr. Felix Hull, archivist to the Kent County Council, they present as complete a record of the times as it is possible to obtain and make fascinating reading. No other copy of these minutes is known to exist.

It is from the record of a meeting held at New Romney in 1570 that we learn:

1. The Bailiffs of the Ports and the Provost of Yarmouth have power of assize during the fair.
2. No one shall bear any armour on him.
3. Every master of a ship or boat is to have his fellowship (i.e. crew) on board between 'the goeing downe of the Sonne unto the Sonne arising'.
4. Ships are only to charge and discharge at Yarmouth on pain of losing the ship, 'wynde and wether force not to the contrarie'.
5. Every baker is to keep the assize of bread and sell four loaves for 1d and one loaf for 1d and every baker to have his 'proper signe on his head'.
6. No taverner of wines shall sell corrupt wine.
7. No brewer shall sell a gallon of the best ale above 2d or of the second above 1d.
8. Taverners and brewers to have their measures sealed.
9. No butcher is to sell unwholesome meat.
10. No cook is to sell unwholesome flesh.
11. No one is to sell by any measure unless it accords with the standard.
12. No forestalling or regrating is to be allowed.

13. No corn is to be sold until the bell in St. Nicholas Church is rung by order of the Bailiffs and Provost on pain of forfeiting all corn.

14. No encroachment shall be made against the 'strond and denn' of the Barons of the Ports of Yarmouth.

From the point of view of the Yarmouth men, the sting is contained in the last item.

There is not space to record the many and varied resolutions adopted by the twin courts, but their wide variety can be estimated by even a cursory glance through the records. One other instance must suffice. It concerns a special Guestling held at New Romney on October 5th 1596, to arrange for the provision of ships against the Dunkirkers. The Speaker was one Nicholas Richardsone of Sandwich. Hastings, Winchelsea, Rye, New Romney, Hythe, Dover, Sandwich, Seaford, Pevensey, Tenterden and Lydd were represented, together with Fordsham, Faversham and Folkstone.

The Mayor of Rye and representatives of Romney, Hythe, Dover, Sandwich, Fordwich and Faversham were appointed to determine 'what nomber of Townes those vj shippes and Pynnice shall bee of which the Ports have offered to her Majestie to suppress her enemyes and what ordinance, powder and shott shall be necessary'.

It was finally decided that five ships and one pinnace should be offered, as follows:

Rye.   1 Ship. 100 tons.
             Powder 1000 weight
             Ordinance: 2 sacres, 4 mynions, 4 falkons,
                         and for every piece 20 shot of
                         all sorts.

Romney.   1 Ship 50 tons.
             Powder 400 weight
             Ordinance: 2 mynions, 4 falkons.
             Shot: 20 of all sorts for each piece.

Hythe.	1 ship 60 tons.
	Powder 500 weight
	Ordinance: 3 mynions, 4 falkons.
	Shot: 20 of all sorts for each piece.
Dover.	1 ship. 80 tons.
	Powder 800 weight
	Ordinance: 4 mynions, 4 falkons.
	Shot. 20 of all sorts for each piece.
Sandwich.	1 Ship. 80 tons.
	Powder, ordinance and shot as for Dover.

There are few references to Naval service in the records, since the arrangements for this comprised the foundation upon which the Confederation was built. In other words these commitments were time honoured and immovable, though there were occasions when the demands made upon the Ports were regarded as onerous and unjust. When this happened a petition to the Lord Warden for the appointment of special solicitors for 'the discharge of this mightie service' would be made, as was the case in 1634 when an order to supply a large ship manned by two hundred and fifty men was received.

Constant bickering between the Portsmen and the Exchequer over the Ports' claim for tax exemption led, in 1594, to an approach to the Lord Warden to ensure that the Ports were granted their rights under an agreement of 1491. The Exchequer disputed the rights claimed, but made no effort to simplify the system.

It was, nevertheless, a situation which could not last indefinitely. Unable to render Naval service in any material sense the Ports still pressed for a recognition of their claims, but by this time they were fighting a losing battle. By the 18th century only one liberty remained intact—one to which the Portsmen clung fiercely as being the outward and visible sign of their privileged status. This was that known as 'Honours at Court'.

From such records as there are available we know that

one of the established rights of the Portsmen was that of carrying a canopy supported by silver staves over the heads of the King and Queen at a Coronation and of being seated at the chief table afterwards in the place of honour on the Monarch's right hand. In 1189 a monk, writing from Christ Church, Canterbury, recorded that 'a pall which belonged by ancient custom to the Barons of Dover and the Cinque Ports on the coronation of the King was offered up . . . on the altar of Christ at Canterbury for an eternal remembrance'. This could, of course, refer only to the Coronation of Richard I. It was customary then, and has been ever since, for the Barons who had attended the Coronation to be given the staves and the silver bells, which were provided by the Lord High Steward, the Barons of Kent giving theirs to Canterbury Cathedral and those of Sussex to Chichester. Later, local churches became the recipients and in one or two instances the staves were retained by individuals to be handed on as family heirlooms.

Quite obviously, the opportunities for the discharge of this duty were not frequent but the privilege was jealously guarded, and while the right to 'honours at court' was confirmed to Hastings alone in the Charter of Henry II, it would seem from subsequent knowledge that no port had precedence over any other.

It is a great pity that we have such scanty records of this important and picturesque ceremony. We do have, however, a most graphic description in the writings of Matthew Paris concerning the Coronation of Henry III and his Queen in 1236. He writes:

'The Barons of the Cinque Ports carried over the King the silken cloth four square, purple, supported by four silvered spears with four silver-gilt bells, four Barons being assigned to every spear according to the diversity of the Ports. Likewise the same Barons bore a silken cloth over the Queen coming after the King which cloths they claim as theirs by right. Moreover the Barons of the Cinque

Ports claimed as theirs the right of sitting at the King's table the same day. And did so sit.'

The first recorded instance of the honours at court being confirmed to all Ports collectively is contained in the Charter of Edward I in 1278 but, as has been stated, the right of all the ports to participate was never in dispute. At each succeeding Coronation claims had to be formally submitted, but there was no question of these not being acknowledged, and in fact the custom was upheld until the reign of George IV. At the Coronation of Richard III in 1483, the claim made then was endorsed by the Lord High Steward, the Duke of Norfolk, his endorsement being subsequently attached to the record book of the Ports kept at Romney. In 1413 Hastings received the canopy carried over Henry V.

The division of the canopy, bells and staves was by arrangement and there seems to have been no disagreement over this until Edward VI was crowned in 1547. Previously it would seem that it had been the practice to divide the canopy between the western and eastern ports alternatively but in 1547 they were, apparently, allocated to Rye. Evidently there was some disagreement about this, for according to the records of the Court of Brotherhood two months later, those who had seized the staves were ordered to hand them over to Rye under pain of a twenty shilling fine.

Another hint of discord came in 1559 when Elizabeth was crowned. There were four claimants to the canopy on this occasion—Dover, Romney, Hastings and Winchelsea —and because of this it was sold for £20 and the money divided.

The King's writ directed to the Lord Warden regarding the services at the Coronation of James I in 1603 ordered him to select men of the 'metest and comlyest among you' and at the assembly of the Ports it was decided that each Baron should wear 'one scarlett gowne, down to the ancle, faced with crymson satten, crymson silk stockings, crymson velvet shoes and black velvet cappes'.

Not all the ceremonies went off smoothly. At the Coronation of Charles II the canopy was seized by the King's footmen when the Barons were about to take their places at the table and but for the prompt intervention of York Herald might have been lost. The King, informed of this happening, sent orders to dismiss the servants and the canopy was handed back to the Barons who, during the fracas, had lost their time honoured places at the King's table. Samuel Pepys witnessed the whole incident and recorded it in his diary. On this occasion, a Coronation Medal engraved by Thomas Simon was struck and distributed.

The first occasion when the claim to dine at the right hand of the King was refused was at the Coronation of William and Mary in 1689 but the canopy was handed over as usual. There had been an earlier break with tradition when James II was crowned. On that occasion the Queen complained that she knew none of the gentlemen who were to bear her canopy, so the bearers had to be changed round, a Colonel Finch serving for Sandwich, Captain Verrier for Hythe, Sir Benjamin Bathhurst for Hastings and a Mr. Milward for Romney. The canopy carried over Queen Anne at her coronation was red with a yellow worsted fringe and was used as a pulpit cloth at All Saints Church in Hastings for many years.

Research has shown that the dress worn by the Barons of the Ports on these various historic occasions varied considerably. We are indebted to Mr. J. Mainwaring Baines, F.S.A., in the Hastings Museum Publication No. 18, for a detailed description of the Baron's dress at the Coronation of George II in 1727. He writes:

'... the robe was made of the finest scarlet cloth, in fashion of a Master of Art's pudding sleeve gown, only a longer train and a large cape, it was faced with rich crimson sarsenet (satin). The waistcoat was of crimson

Sandwich, St. Clement's Church Tower

sarsenet, faced white sarsenet, the Breeches of the same cloth with the robe. The stockings were of the finest scarlet worsted. The shoes were black velvet, the cap the same, in fashion of a Scotch bonnet, with a ribbon on it to hang on his arm, full bottom wigs, neckcloth and ruffles of the finest lace and white gloves faced with crimson sarsenet. They all wore swords and some had very fine sword knots'.

The Hastings Barons pooled their shares of the staves and bells and had a silver punch bowl made which they presented to the Corporation. It weighs one hundred and sixty-four ounces, measures sixteen inches in diameter and holds about four gallons. The hallmarks show the maker to have been Joseph Bird, of London 1727–1728. Around the bowl are two inscriptions which are of great interest in that Hastings' claim to be the premier port is noted. Between them are the figures of George II and Queen Caroline, both crowned and robed and holding orbs and sceptres.

In his book, Mr. Baines describes how, when George IV was crowned, the Barons came very near to losing their canopy altogether. He quotes the following account:

'The Philistines were upon the precious treasure and were hacking off odd bits. The Barons, making a gallant rush, scattered them and seizing what was left of the canopy, carried it into the sanctuary. This was first sought in the House of Commons but manoeuvre as they might they could not get the thing through the doorway. It found shelter at last in the House of Lords. They were up bright and early the next morning and conveyed the canopy to the Thatched House and divided the spoil. The rich purple silk, the gold cloth and the framework of the canopy were divided into sixteen parts, one assigned to each of the sixteen barons. They drew lots for the silver staves and bells.'

This was, sadly, the last occasion when the canopy was borne by the Barons. William IV dispensed with the

Brookland Church Bell Tower

procession so that the Portsmen would have no duties to perform in the Abbey. On the next occasion, the Coronation of Queen Victoria, the claim of the Cinque Ports was rejected on the same grounds, and for a time it seemed that one of England's most picturesque and ancient customs was lost. Shortly before the Coronation of Edward VII, however, at a Brotherhood and Guestling held at Hastings, it was decided to reassert the time honoured right of the Ports to take part. As a result, the Earl Marshal was directed to reserve places in the Abbey for eighteen Barons, a procedure which was followed at the Coronation of George V, George VI, and the present Queen. No canopy has been carried by the Barons since the Coronation of George IV in 1821.

CHAPTER III

Heraldry

In the days when King John, Edward I and Henry II endorsed the rights and privileges of the Cinque Ports in return for ship service they did much more than ratify a loosely constructed agreement between king and subjects. They were recognising a basic strategic fact, namely that he who holds the Cinque Ports holds the gateway of England.

It was a fact that was driven home to Prince Edward during the Baron's War, when the Portsmen backed de Montfort and virtually closed the Channel against the King. It was no doubt primarily responsible for the charter by which Edward, soon after he became King in 1272 breathed fresh life into the Confederation and gave it a status it had previously lacked.

Earlier, the sudden death of King John (1216) left the insurgent barons who had risen against him in a quandary. They had called Louis of France to their aid and were now faced with the realisation that they had made a mistake. John's successor was his eldest son Henry, a boy of nine, who was immediately crowned King at Gloucester by the Earl of Pembroke, one of the barons who had refused to join Louis. Pembroke caused the young King to republish the Great Charter, and in so doing cut away the ground from under the rebels' feet, as they could no longer pretend they were fighting for their constitutional rights.

The civil war continued but the tide gradually turned in favour of the King. Finally, any hopes of victory entertained by Louis were shattered by the Portsmen! He was expecting reinforcements from France, to be brought over in a fleet commanded by Eustace the Monk. Hubert de Burgh put to sea from Dover with a squadron of ships raised from the Cinque Ports and met the Frenchmen off Sandwich. Victory was with the English who sank large numbers of the French vessels, and Eustace the Monk was taken and hanged for piracy. This was the first major engagement won by an English fleet at sea and was responsible for a complete reappraisal of the status and importance of the Ports.

As a result of all this the Cinque Ports found their liberties more firmly entrenched than ever, amounting in fact to a loose form of self government. It did not require this to underline the independence, even the lawlessness of the Portsmen, but their importance in maintaining the freedom of the Channel was great enough to ensure that even their predisposition to piracy was overlooked.

Sandwich, Doorway of the Ancient Guildhall with the arms of the Ports

Just when the status of the Ports became embodied in the use of heraldic arms it is difficult to say. One thing is certain, the Ports were using arms long before there existed such an institution as the College of Heralds which is, no doubt, why we can find no grant registered there. The only positive evidence of the antiquity of the Cinque Ports arms rests in the records of the Confederation itself, but even here we find conflict. From this, therefore, we are led inescapably to the only reliable source from which something like a true picture can be obtained—the common seals of the Ports themselves.

One of the earliest of these is undoubtedly that of Dover. This depicts a ship flying an heraldic banner bearing the device we have come to accept as the arms of the Confederation—three lions passant joined to three ships' hulls. Confirmation is provided by the common seal of Hastings which displays two ships in conflict, one of which is flying two ensigns. One of these is identical to that of the Dover seal. It would seem, from this, that the device of three lions subjoined to three ships was not confined to one particular port but was, in fact, common to the majority of the towns involved.

The device itself is one that is known as dimidiated, that is, a process of amalgamation dating from the beginning of the 14th century. W. St. John Hope states that the earliest municipal arms known to him to which a definite date can be attached are those of Chester, which occur on a seal of 1283 and represent the three lions of England combined with the three golden garbs of the Earldom of Chester. He adds that 'of about the same time, since they occur on the dated Dover seal are the singular arms borne by . . . the Cinque Ports and their dependencies'.

The seals of the Ports are among the oldest corporate ones known. Nearly all display the common factor of a single masted vessel but there are a number of puzzling differences. The Hastings seal depicting two ships in combat would seem to indicate that the English vessel was flying both the Royal standard and the banner of the Cinque Ports, a reminder of the Convention of Bruges in 1297 when it was agreed that English ships sailing into Flemish waters should display *'le signal des armes du Roy d'Angleterre'*.

The seals of Winchelsea, Rye and Pevensey bear moons, stars and suns over their vessels. Geoffrey Williams in his *Heraldry of the Cinque Ports* surmises that these are crusading symbols, for while their limited size would render the ships depicted on the seals unsuited to long voyages they could well have been used for transportation to and from the Continent. This theory finds considerable support when it is remembered that Edward I was a patron of Rye and Winchelsea and personally drew the town plans for the rebuilding of the latter. He took part in a Crusade before his Coronation in 1274. As each town was granted a charter by Richard I on his way to the Holy Land in 1191 it seems safe to assume that the seals in question are copies of earlier ones which commemorate that occasion.

There does not seem to have been a common seal used by the Confederation as such. The only Confederation seal about which there is any positive evidence is that of the Cinque Ports' bailiffs who attended at Great Yarmouth. Even so we do not know when a seal for the bailiffs came into being, for while there are numerous references in the White and Black Books to the sealing of documents it seems likely that the seal used on such occasions would have been that of the member town where a meeting took place.

A small amount of light is thrown on the subject by a resolution of the Court of Brotherhood in 1613 which suggests that, until then, no common seal of any kind existed. The resolution runs:

'It is ordered . . . that a seal specially engraven with the Ports' armes shall be commended to the successive

Bayliffs to Great Yermouth and by them used to enseal
all passports warrants and precepts concerning the said
office and the same shall be delivered from Bayliffe to
Bayliffee with the box of Yermouth books and banner.'

Further to this it should be remembered that the
Cinque Ports were boroughs by prescription and it was
not until very much later that the right to have and to
use a seal was included in the Charter of Incorporation.
Before this each of the Ports had adopted and used a
common seal. The inscriptions on many of these seals
are unusual, those of the head ports being of Lombardic
character which would indicate their introduction before
the middle of the 14th century. Those which date from
the 15th century and later, show a return to the Roman
style.

It would not be fitting in a survey of this kind, to
exclude Great Yarmouth. The Norfolk fishing port was
never a member of the Confederation but its long and
sometimes bloody association with the Ports, lasting from
before the Conquest to 1663 gives it a place in their
history to which it is fully entitled.

The town's first common seal depicts a ship with an
embattled forecastle and poop. Of particular interest is the
illustration of a square fighting top forward of the single
mast. Two men are shown upon the yardarm, and below,
a trumpeter on the aftercastle. The inscription reads
SICILLVM COMVNITATIS DE CERNEMVTHAE.

The bailiff's seal went out of use when the office of
Bailiff was replaced by that of Mayor in 1684.

The post of Constable of Dover Castle was a purely
military post, while that of the Lord Warden was a
temporary appointment brought into being when necessary, as for example, when the monarch required the
services of the ports. Later, however, when the two
offices were combined in the early middle ages, it would
seem that the Lord Warden was given the right to his

A Winchelsea Seal *Photo [Edward Reeves]*

A Winchelsea Seal   *Photo [Edward Reeves]*

own personal standard. Very little reference is made to this in early records, but Lord Curzon has described how, when William Pitt reviewed a fleet of vessels from the Cinque Ports in 1803 the warden's flag was acknowledged by the ships anchored off Walmer Castle.

Two examples of the flag are still in existence. One is in the care of the registrar of the Ports, at Dover. Due to the fact that the office of Lord Warden is now merely nominal, the occasions on which the flag would be likely to be displayed are not frequent. It is worthy of note, however, that during Sir Winston Churchill's funeral procession in January 1965, a replica of the banner of the Cinque Ports preceded the coffin and when the launch *Havengore* bore his body from Tower Pier to Waterloo, the flag of the Lord Warden was flown from the jackstaff.

CHAPTER IV

The Ports of Sandwich, Deal and Walmer

Sandwich

It is hard to believe, today, that Sandwich was once one of the most important of the Cinque Ports. Left over two miles inland by the receding sea, it is no longer a great port and trading centre, a favoured landing place for travellers from the Continent. At that time the Wantsum Channel separated the Isle of Thanet from the mainland, with Reculver at its northern end. Where the ruins of Richborough Castle now stand, the armies of the Emperor Claudius landed in AD 43, and because of its strategic position, the Romans built a fort there, establishing their first and most important base and supply centre in Britain.

The Roman fort (Rutupiae) later became one of the line of Roman forts described in Chapter I. While the ancient town of Stonar across the Wantsum remained a place of quite considerable importance, Sandwich was already being developed. The first recorded mention of it as a port and landing place tells us that in 644, St. Wilfred, returning from France came ashore 'in Sandwich Haven'. Before the Conquest Sandwich was granted to the Priory of Christchurch in Canterbury and for many years remained a possession of Christchurch. It paid an annual rent of £40 to Canterbury to which was added a yearly contribution of forty thousand herrings! This state of affairs lasted until the mid-13th century when the monastic ownership of the port was ended. The first mayor was elected in 1226.

As one of the chief ports of arrival and departure at that time, Sandwich welcomed and bade farewell to a great number of prominent persons. It was from Sandwich that Thomas Becket departed to exile in France. An account from the Chronicle of Allan of Tewkesbury relates how Becket waited hidden in the manor of Eastry for some days before it was considered safe for him to venture out. Six years later he returned, landing at Sandwich harbour on the first day of December 1170 and here the crowds turned out to welcome him. He little knew it then but his time was running out, for it was only three days after Christmas that his murderers met in secret at Saltwood Castle to complete their plans for the following day.

Among others who landed at Sandwich were Richard I, who stepped ashore there after his safe return from imprisonment in Austria, and Edward of Woodstock, called

Sandwich, The river today

45

the Black Prince, in 1357. A landing of a very different kind took place almost a century later, when a force of four thousand French sacked the town and killed the mayor, John Drury. The black robe worn by the Mayor of Sandwich, and the black bows which adorn his chain of office, are traditionally worn in mourning for the murdered man. With the exception of Deal, whose mayor wears a black robe with gold trimmings as befitting a Corporate Member of Sandwich, all the mayors of the Cinque Ports wear red.

By the middle of the 16th century Sandwich had already begun to decline in importance. The sea was receding and the harbour silting up, and for the next hundred years the records tell of the long, losing fight to save the situation. Appeals to the Crown for help gained very little, though Henry VIII visited the town and promised the money so sorely needed. This was not forthcoming, and in the end it was suggested that funds for the reconstruction of the harbour should be raised from the sale of ornaments and plate in the possession of the three parish churches. Still later, Queen Elizabeth was prevailed upon to pay the town a visit, but despite the lavish decorations arranged in her honour nothing emerged from it all despite the promises that were made to the Mayor and Council.

Nevertheless, the Queen's patronage achieved a result not quite foreseen by those who arranged her visit. During her stay she expressed concern for the well-being of Protestants from France and the Netherlands who had fled to England to escape religious persecution. This did much to reconcile the people of Sandwich to an influx which, as it happened, proved to be the salvation of the town. As might have been expected, the newcomers introduced fresh skills and trades, including market gardening and the production of serge, and in less than half a century Sandwich had been transformed from a dying port into a thriving market town.

Sandwich, Ship's figurehead on the bank of the Stour

Some of the Flemish architecture dating from that time can be seen in the older buildings which remain, like lingering ghosts, to remind us of the vanished past.

Today, you can walk almost completely round the town by way of the ancient ramparts, now merely grass covered banks, many of the stretches bearing names that carry us back to the 14th and 15th centuries; Plague Field, where those afflicted were set aside and then buried; the Tannery and the Rope Walk; and, most romantic of all, the Butts where, it is said, some of Henry V's archers practised their skill. William Boys lived in White Friars which gained its name from a monastic house of the Carmelites founded on the site in 1272. Other sections are the Mill Wall, the Bulwark and the Watergate entrance from the Isle of Thanet.

In the ancient Guildhall there are two Cinque Ports relics; the original Charter granted by Charles II and part of the Canopy borne by the Barons of the Cinque Ports at the Coronation of George III in 1761. The Mayoral Chair was made in 1561 and with its elaborately carved arm rests is probably one of the finest examples of its kind in England.

One of the oldest traditions in Sandwich is the carrying by the Mayor of a Wand of Office. This consists of a very straight blackthorn stick which is produced each year for the new Mayor by the Town Sergeant, in exchange for which he is given a coin by the Mayor to the value of a crown. Supposed to protect the Mayor against witches, these blackthorn sticks are carried on every civic occasion. Each mayor keeps his stick at the end of his term of office but whether it still retains its magic properties afterwards is not known.

On Mayor's Sunday the Mayor and Corporation walk in procession from the Guildhall to St. Clement's Church. The Norman tower of the church is a well known Sandwich landmark, which dates from approximately 1100. Among other colourful ceremonies is one which takes place in July of each year, when those who have to be sworn in as Mayor Deputy of each member town come to Sandwich to pay their Ship Money. Each Deputy is handed his chain of office, among which the Brightlingsea chain is specially fine, composed of crossed silver fishes and oyster shells, with a medallion containing one of the largest opals in the world.

Another of the traditional customs celebrated each year is that of 'St. Barts. Day' when the new Master of St. Bartholomews Hospital is 'pricked out' by the Chairman of the Trustees. From a list of the men of the almshouses the Master is selected by pricking his name with a bodkin, after which the Mayor and Trustees file out into the courtyard where the children of Sandwich race for the Bartlesmas Bun. The course goes round the Chapel and the winner gets a St. Barts Biscuit, while the rest get sticky buns!

Sandwich possesses two other churches of great antiquity—St. Peter's, where Thomas Paine, author of *The Rights of Man*, was married, and St. Mary's. St. Peter's was built during the reign of King John but has suffered a great deal of damage, and consequent restoration, during the succeeding centuries. The tower collapsed in 1661.

St. Mary's in Strand Street has a rare survival of ancient times in Peter's Pence Box, which was once used for the collection of the Papal Tribute. The collection of Peter's Pence was abolished by Henry VIII and the relic in St. Mary's is very rare indeed.

Punishments for wrongdoing in days gone by were harsh by any standard, but amongst the Cinque Ports, Sandwich must take the palm for the most grisly of them all. In Gallows Field, close to the site of the old Canterbury Gate, criminals were buried alive! Nearby is the Guestling Stream where anyone convicted of witchcraft was drowned.

Ramsgate, Deal and Walmer were member towns. Brightlingsea is the only town in the Confederation which is not located in Kent or Sussex. Pegwell Bay, from where a cross-Channel hovercraft service now operates is where Hengist and Horsa are reputed to have landed in AD 449 and not far away is Ebbsfleet, where St. Augustine came ashore in AD 597. Eastry is not far away, and legend tells us that there was a palace of the Kentish kings here in the 7th century. There is no trace of it now, though the site is believed to be where Eastry Court now stands. There is a very fine church, dedicated to St. Mary the Virgin, which dates from the early 13th century and must therefore have succeeded the Norman church where Thomas Becket took refuge. The chapel where he was able to look through a hole in the wall, and share in the celebration of the mass without being observed, is no longer there but one cannot step down into the great nave, with its magnificent roof high above without being reminded of H. V. Morton's idea of stored up centuries. One of the treasures of the church is a copy of the Vinegar Bible, so called because the printer, John Baskett, in setting up the heading to the Gospel of St. Luke, Chapter XX, made it read 'The Parable of the Vinegar' instead of 'The Parable of the Vineyard'.

Today the Stour is a peaceful, secluded stream meandering between reedy banks, bearing nothing more important than a small yacht or a sailing dinghy making its way upstream. Yet town and river combine, in some mysterious way, to remind us of the time when Sandwich played its part in shaping the history of England, and at night, when the traffic has dwindled to a mere trickle, one can walk through the twisted, narrow streets past shuttered houses, and imagine the Watch coming round a corner, lantern hanging from a pole, while the guardians of public safety peer into dark corners for whatever luckless wretch might be hiding there.

Deal and Walmer

Deal and Walmer were both non-corporate members of the Confederation and are so ranked in the Charter of Charles II in 1668. Yet their strategic importance became intensified with the decline of Sandwich as a port, occupying as they did a vital stretch of coast line which included the important naval anchorage known as the Downs. In addition, from the early 18th century Walmer Castle has been the official home of the Lords Warden of the Cinque Ports.

Their castles are castles by courtesy only. Visitors looking for the traditional Norman 'motte and bailey' castle, with its barbican and massive keep, are likely to be disappointed. Built by order of Henry VIII, they were designed purely as gun-platforms and served much the same purpose as the much later Martello towers. They were part of a chain of similar fortresses built along the coast against the possibility of invasion from the Continent, the threat of which arose as a result of Henry's

Deal Castle, one of Henry VIII's *Tudor Rose* Castles

defiance of the Pope. After Henry's excommunication in
1538 the Pope endeavoured to enlist the aid of the Holy
Roman Emperor Charles V in an attack aimed at restoring
England to the Papal fold. The invasion never material-
ised, but at the time the threat was a very real one and
Henry was taking no chances. Gunfire had become a new
and dominant factor in Naval warfare and it had already
been established that a stable gun platform such as that
provided by Deal and Walmer were extremely effective
against a seaborne landing.

At Walmer the austere lines of the fort have been
modified by the planting of formal gardens and trees, as
well as by windows and new roof lines which result from
the alterations considered necessary to convert it into a
suitable residence for the Lords Warden. Whereas at
Deal, the exterior is as uncompromising as ever. Eastwards
across the four miles of sheltered water lie the Goodwin
Sands. Ships still anchor there in bad weather. On at
least one occasion in the last century over five hundred
sail were counted waiting for a favourable wind! At the
time of the Armada the main body of the English fleet
was based there and it was from Deal and Walmer that
the fireships were sent out to scatter and demoralise the
Spanish force sheltering in Calais roads. It was on Walmer
beach that Julius Caesar landed in 55 BC and it was from
Deal that Blake set out to join battle with de Witt and
the Dutch fleet.

Although the coastal defences built by Henry VIII
were not the first designed with artillery as the dominant
weapon in mind, they were nevertheless revolutionary.
They were revolutionary in the sense that they ignored
the older conventions of castle building and heralded the
acceptance of an entirely new concept of war. Planned
with four large circular bastions around the small central
keep, they had a wide, deep moat and parapets curved to
deflect gunshots. The main armament was mounted on
the outer and inner bastions and on top of the keep. At

Walmer Castle, Moat Garden

Sandown and Walmer there were casemates in the outer bastions to make it possible to enfilade the moat and both moat and courtyard were protected by openings for handguns.

Originally there were massive earthworks linking the castles. They have now vanished, as have those linking Deal and Sandown, but from old drawings it would seem that there were also trenches for communication between the fortifications. Slight variations in the design of these 'castles' can be found at Sandgate and Camber, where the latter has four bastions and a gatehouse bastion, but the basic idea is manifest in the plan of all of them—that is, a virtually impregnable fortress built around a central keep.

The stone from which the castles were built came from local quarries and the seashore. Further supplies were obtained from disused religious houses, among them Christchurch and Canterbury. Other supplies were obtained from the Carmelite Friary at Sandwich, which explains the presence of Caen stone in the walls. Masons were brought from as far afield as Somerset, and it is recorded that at Sandgate, for example, the total labour force engaged there in 1540 was over six hundred.

Skilled men received 7d. or 8d. a day and labourers 5d. or 6d. Any hint of industrial unrest was dealt with summarily. When the labourers struck at Deal for 6d. a day in 1539, the leaders were imprisoned—five being sent to Canterbury and four to Sandwich jail.

The armament of the castles varied a great deal and frequent changes took place. At the beginning of the 16th century bows and arrows remained in use but were gradually displaced by the arquebus on a fixed support used mainly in the embrasures covering the moat and courtyard. Early guns were on the large side, being great 'bombards' similar to the 'Mons Meg' still to be seen at Edinburgh Castle, but they in turn gave way to the more easily handled and considerably more accurate 32-pounders—the demi-cannon—and the culverin, with its 5-inch bore and 18-pound shot. Ranges were surprisingly good—about a mile and a half for the cannon and just over a mile for the culverin. Considering the virtual impregnability of the defences and the total weight of their armament, it can be seen that for an enemy to occupy the Downs anchorage and effect a landing the guns would have to be silenced first.

Deal and Walmer castles were besieged during the Civil War. Both, together with Sandown, had been in Parliamentary hands but later Sandown declared for the King and both Deal and Walmer capitulated shortly afterwards. Finally all three were retaken by a force under Colonel Rich who set out to relieve Dover Castle with two thousand foot and horse and then moved on to the Downs.

Despite the fact the castles were never used for the purpose for which they were intended they played an important part by acting as a deterrent. During the Napoleonic wars they were kept in a state of readiness, and Cinque Ports' volunteers built earthen fortifications.

Of Sandown virtually nothing remains. Sea erosion and a fire ended attempts to save it in 1856 and demolition was ordered. Some of the stones used in additions to the gatehouse at Walmer came from Sandown. It was in Sandown that Colonel Hutchinson, the regicide, was imprisoned after the Restoration and even then it had evidently fallen on evil days, for his wife complained that it was a 'lamentable old ruined place'.

As stated earlier, the Lord Wardenship began in the 13th century and by the reign of Edward I the post had become one of permanent authority. It was a life appointment and carried a handsome salary, so there was a great deal of competition for the honour. Although the office has become a nominal one, the salary having ceased in 1828, the Lord Warden's position has been compared with that of a Lord Lieutenant. Nevertheless, Walmer Castle has been the official residence of the Lords Warden since 1708, when rooms were built out from the keep by the first Duke of Dorset, the first resident Warden.

Walmer has housed many famous and distinguished

Walmer Castle, the Entrance Walk

55

Walmer Castle, Battlements

figures and in a great many cases they have left their mark. During the years of William Pitt's office (1792–1806) Lady Hester Stanhope, his niece, did a great deal to improve the gardens, but credit for the present layout goes to Lord Granville (1865–1891) who also added several rooms above the gatehouse.

Queen Victoria stayed at Walmer in 1835 when only sixteen years old and in 1842 she stayed there for a month with the Prince Consort and their two eldest children. This makes nonsense of the story told by Lord Curzon (1903–1905) that the Queen left the castle after one night there, complaining that her bed was damp.

Walmer still preserves the room Pitt used as a study, as well as the room in which the Duke of Wellington lived and died. One cannot stand in the barely furnished, austere apartment without being deeply moved, redolent as it is of the Spartan character of the man who so richly deserved the title of The Iron Duke. The armchair in which he died in 1852 still stands there, the upholstery

Walmer Castle, Cannon with shot

faded, together with the narrow camp bed he used on all his campaigns. A friend of his once expressed surprise to find him using a bed on which there was no room to turn and was told 'When one begins to turn in bed it is time to turn out'. In the centre of the room is a high desk, at which he used to work standing up!

Deal was granted a new coat of arms in 1966, the shield bearing the three demi-lions passant and the three demi-hulls of the Cinque Ports surmounted by a silver oar. The oar, carried before the Mayor on ceremonial occasions is a symbol of his special status which confers the rank of Admiral on him whenever he visits a ship of the Royal Navy lying off-shore.

CHAPTER V

The Ports of Dover, Hythe, New Romney, Lydd and Dymchurch

Dover

Dominated by the great castle on the heights above the town, Dover incorporates in its history all that is noteworthy since the time when the vast earthworks above the sea were first raised to make an Iron Age fort. From that time, to the present day, the strategic and historical importance of Dover has never been seriously challenged. The Romans occupied the site in the first century, building their *pharos* or lighthouse, next to which is the Saxon church of St. Mary-in-Castro built nearly a thousand years later.

The reasons for the importance of Dover are twofold. The virtual impregnability of the site and the vulnerability of the harbour combine to make the latter completely dependent upon the former, a fact recognised by all. A key point in the Norman Conquest, it commands the shortest route to the Continent and unlike the rest of the Cinque Ports, Dover still represents 'The Gateway of England', and must be rendered ineffective before an enemy could establish a bridgehead.

The town's importance is underlined by the fact that when appeals from other ports for help fell on deaf ears, as in the case of Sandwich, the Tudors answered Dover's cry for help, responding generously when a massive cliff fall blocked the harbour. In the reign of Henry VIII an embankment was built to form a protective barrier to the sea. Queen Elizabeth did a great deal and with her support a new harbour was built, the forerunner of the harbour we know today.

A pageant of history unfolds before anyone seeking to turn back the clock. It was from Dover that Richard I left for the Third Crusade, and it was here that King John, bowing to the inevitable, knelt before Pandulf, the Papal legate, to surrender to the Church of Rome and Pope Innocent the Third, the Kingdoms of England and Ireland together with all the rights belonging to them. It was from Dover that Hubert de Burgh set out with the Cinque Ports' fleet to defeat the French in the great sea battle of Sandwich, a battle which put an end to the hopes of the Dauphin Louis in 1216.

One of the other great occasions in the history of the port was the departure of Henry VIII for his meeting with François I of France at the Field of the Cloth of Gold. Accompanied by Thomas Wolsey, Cardinal of York, Charles, Duke of Suffolk, the Archbishop of Canterbury, the Duke of Buckingham and many others bearing illustrious titles, the King was conveyed across the Channel by a fleet of Cinque Ports' ships. The official

The Pharos (Roman Lighthouse), at Dover, with St. Mary's-in-Castro

record tells us that 'never in the memory of man was seen so vast a multitude so bravely arrayed and adorned'.

Other famous arrivals and departures are recorded in Dover's history. Charles II landed at Dover on his return from exile, and was presented by the Mayor with a Bible. Bleriot, the first man to fly to England from the Continent in 1909, landed in a meadow close to the castle, the place marked for ever by the white outlines of an aeroplane in the grass. It was an epic flight and inspired, in one of the leading newspapers of the day, the prophetic headline 'Great Britain no longer an island'!

Plans for the evacuation of the British Army from Dunkirk were formulated in Dover Castle and if anything in modern times echoes the role of the Cinque Ports it was this, for there was scarcely a creek or an inlet which did not contribute its quota of small craft to this miraculous and selfless rescue.

It is the Castle which always dominates, however. The first Norman castle was a fortification which came into being soon after the battle of Hastings. This was replaced by Henry II who paid out very large sums of money for the construction of a massive keep and the inner bailey's walls and towers. Additions were made by Richard I and King John, but it was left to Henry III to embark on an extensive building programme which included the Constable's Tower, still the principal entrance to the castle.

When the invention of siege cannon rendered the conventional medieval castle obsolete, many were abandoned and fell into ruin, or became quarries for building stone, which was always in short supply. Dover Castle, however, because of its strategic importance escaped this fate. In fact, more than ordinary care and maintenance was lavished on it and Edward IV is said to have spent £10,000 on the keep alone. In the Tudor period, wars with France occasioned further work. Mary Tudor rebuilt the tower which is now named after her.

The Roman Pharos, Dover

In the official guide to the castle there is a list of some of the more notable constables of the castle. It includes Odo, Bishop of Bayeux, half-brother of the Conqueror and, of course Stephen de Pencestre. Others were Henry, Prince of Wales (1409–1413) afterwards Henry V, and Henry, Duke of York (afterwards Henry VIII.)

The Statutes of Dover Castle were drawn up by Stephen de Pencestre, who was the first holder of the combined office of Constable and Lord Warden of the Cinque Ports. Most of them concern defence, garrison duties and religious observances, but there are amongst them some which are decidedly unusual. It was laid down that:

> . . . if a Chief Guard discovers a Warder asleep he shall take something from him as he lies or carry away his staff or cut a piece out of part of his clothes to witness against him in case the Warder should deny having been asleep and he shall lose his day's wage.

Bad language was also frowned upon and a Sergeant or a Warden found guilty of using it was brought up before the Constable and could lose a day's pay.

A quaint regulation obviously designed as a precaution against possible treachery by impersonation forbade the opening of the main gates after dark had fallen. The statute lays down that:

> If the King arrives unexpectedly in the night, the gates shall not be opened to him, but he shall go to the postern called the King's Gate where the Constable . . . may admit the King and a member of his suite.

The castle has served as a royal residence throughout its long and colourful history and a visitor cannot walk around without being reminded of the many occasions when a royal bride was first introduced to the man whose wife she was destined to be. It was in Dover Castle that Richard II met Anne of Bohemia, in probably the same

Entrenchments, Dover Castle

courtyard where Isabella—the 'She Wolf of France'—was shown to his assembled courtiers by Edward II. Charles I greeted Henrietta Maria of France here, at a time when they could not possibly have had any foreboding of the troubled and tragic times that lay ahead.

The oldest buildings on the hill are the Church of St. Mary-in-Castro and the Roman *pharos*. The latter is believed to date from the 1st century AD. The construction is curious, for it is octagonal without and rectangular within. It rose to a height of some eighty feet through eight stages, each stepped about one foot back from the one below. Only the first four of the Roman stages now remain. When the church was built the *pharos* became the bell tower!

There are numerous underground works, some, at the northern end of the castle, constructed by Hubert de Burgh in the early 13th century. Later they were extended, in an attempt to bring the defences up to date during the Napoleonic wars. The object was to enable the garrison to reach, under cover, important defensive positions such as the great outwork thrown up before the castle.

As far as can be ascertained, there is nothing to show that the defences of the castle were adapted for the use of guns during the later Middle Ages. Henry VIII was responsible for artillery fortifications intended as a protection for the newly enlarged harbour. They took the form of small blockhouses holding batteries, such as the Moat's Bulwark, below the castle cliff, but were in no sense a strengthening of the castle defences.

A 12-pounder gun cast in Utrecht in 1544 by Jan Tolhuys was presented by the Emperor Charles V to Henry VIII, and it is known to have been mounted at Dover Castle in 1613. Known as Queen Elizabeth's Pocket Pistol, it is of unusual length, 24 feet, with a calibre of 4.75 inches and it is reputed to be able to throw a ball some seven miles! During the Civil War it was used by the Parliamentarians at the siege of Sheffield.

In Dover, a building with a very special significance in any record of the Confederation is the Maison Dieu. It was founded by Hubert de Burgh in 1203 as a hostel for pilgrims arriving from the Continent on their way to Canterbury. Later, sick and wounded soldiers returning from the wars were taken in and in a few instances, permanent pensioners were lodged there. Henry VIII brought the institution to an end in 1544.

The building, in a sad state of disrepair, was bought by the Dover Corporation in 1834. Restored by Ambrose Poynter and William Burgess, it now houses an imposing collection of portraits of Lords Warden of the Cinque Ports and is also the repository for the original banner of the Ports used each year at the opening of the Yarmouth Herring Fair.

Not far away is the lovely little chapel of St. Edmund. Dating from the 13th century, the chapel was consecrated by St. Richard of Chichester in 1253 a few days before he died in the Maison Dieu. Thus, Dover possesses the only standing chapel in England consecrated by one English canonised saint in honour of another. St. Richard knew, loved and venerated St. Edmund so that the chapel stands today as a memorial to them both.

The remains of the Knights Templar's Church on the Western Heights were excavated early in the 19th century. The church is not only one of the smallest in the country but is one of the very few round church sites left in England. The Court of Shepway met here at one time but is now only called together for the installation of a new Lord Warden, the proceedings being held in the grounds of Dover College.

The installation of a new Lord Warden and Constable of Dover Castle is an important and colourful ceremony. It begins at the castle where the new Lord Warden is handed the key of the castle by the Deputy Constable. The church service which follows is held in the church of St. Mary-in-Castro and thereafter the installation

Dover Castle, view from the Keep

St. Leonard's Church, Hythe

ceremonial of the Court of Shepway is conducted in a marquee in the Priory Close of Dover College. Normally the 17th-century silver oar, symbol of authority of the Cinque Ports, is carried before the Warden by the Sergeant of Admiralty and was so carried at the installation of the present Lord Warden, Sir Robert Menzies. It was stolen when Dover Museum was burgled and has not been recovered. It has been replaced by a replica.

Hythe

Hythe is mentioned in Domesday where it is described as part of the manor of Saltwood with 255 burgesses. Among the town's most treasured possessions is the Charter of Edward I, setting out, for the Confederation as a whole, the obligations and privileges contained in earlier, individual charters. On a grassy mound beside the road from Hythe to Lympne stands a tall, ornamental cross—The Shepway Cross.

This marks the traditional meeting place of the ancient Court of Shepway. Meetings outside on horseback were a common event in the Middle Ages. At Dover there is a report of a meeting of the Court at the Shepway cross-roads in 1358, presided over by Roger Mortimer, Earl of March, and attended by sixty-five Barons of the Cinque Ports.

Unfortunately, due to the changes in the coastline that have occurred since the days when Hythe was a founder member of the Confederation, it is no longer a port, the natural harbour, formed by a creek which cut inland to West Hythe, now being silted up. Shingle has accumulated to extend the foreshore so that today a large part of the town is built upon land formerly covered by the sea. No trace of the creek or the old harbour remains.

Apart from the role it played as a member of the Cinque Ports Confederation, the history of Hythe goes back a long way. It was in Canute's reign that the manor of Saltwood, of which Hythe formed a part was granted to Christchurch in Canterbury. Later it passed to Lanfranc, first Norman archbishop of Canterbury. Hythe and Saltwood became the property of the Crown during the reign of Henry VIII. It was not until 1575 that the Charter of Elizabeth I gave the town control over its own affairs.

It seems strange that Hythe did not, apparently, suffer from the frequent raids and sackings by the French, which beset many of the other ports, Rye and Winchelsea in particular. It suffered in other ways, however. The Black Death (1348–1349) took a devastating toll of the population and, fifty years later, the plague further reduced the town to a shadow of its former self.

Fires were almost an occupational hazard to the people of those days, living as they did in closely packed timber and thatched cottages, and violent storms, often resulting in great loss of life, lent support to a growing belief that the town was accursed. During Henry IV's reign a movement to leave and build afresh on new ground, like Winchelsea, might have gained ground if the King had not released Hythe from ship service until such time as the port had recovered from its disasters.

The old town, clinging to a steep hillside half a mile inland, is dominated by the parish church of St. Leonard. Built in the early 12th century, it was much enlarged in 1165. The chancel, built in 1220 is very lofty and is approached by a flight of nine steps and has both a triforium and a clerestory. The church registers are stored in an iron chest whose main lock is linked with a series of eleven bolts so heavy that a lever is needed to turn the key.

An intriguing field of study for the antiquarian is presented by the collection of thigh bones and skulls in the ancient ambulatory, now the crypt. It is said there are about 8,000 thigh bones and 1,500 skulls, dating from around the early 13th century. We are told on unimpeachable authority that the skulls differ from British types, and numerous theories have been advanced to account for this. One, considered to be the most acceptable is that they are the skulls of descendants of the Romano-British left behind when the Romans departed. There are few signs of wounds or injury among them, suggesting that the deaths were natural and it may be that when the plague made excessive demands upon the available burial ground the bones were removed and placed where they are today. In the churchyard a visitor will find the grave of Lionel Lukin, the inventor of the lifeboat.

One small item of interest in the church is the Motorists' Prayer. The author is unknown, but one could wish that motoring organisations would print it on all their literature. It runs:

> Give me a steady hand, a watchful eye,
> That none may suffer hurt when I pass by.
> Thou givest life: I pray no act of mine

May take away or mar that gift of Thine.
Shield those, dear Lord, who bear me company,
From foolish folk and all calamity.
Teach me to use my car for others' need.
Let me not miss through witless love of speed
The beauties of Thy world. That thus I may
With joy and courtesy go on my way.

Hythe can boast two castles which are the very stuff of
history. They are Saltwood Castle, on the northern peri-
meter of the town and Lympne Castle built high on the
edge of the inland cliff which faces west over the marsh.
Both are of great antiquity and both belonged to Canterbury, for Saltwood was a residence for archbishops and
Lympne for archdeacons. Both castles today are in private
ownership.

It was in Saltwood Castle that the assassination of
Thomas à Becket was planned. He had lived at Lympne as
an archdeacon and later at Saltwood as archbishop,
before he was forced to escape to France. A question no
historian can answer with any degree of certainty is that
which comes to mind from Henry II's petulant outburst
when he asked, 'Who will rid me of this meddlesome
priest?' All we know is that it sent four knights hurrying
from his court to commit a crime, the horror of which
still rings down through the corridors of time.

Lympne Castle is superbly situated. From it on a fine
day, with a few fleecy clouds drifting across the sky it is
possible to stand for hours watching the changing light
vary the different shades of sea green from pure emerald
to ultramarine.

Looking around, it is easy to picture the scene as it
must have been when the Romano-British fleet patrolled
the shore line and a Roman watch tower stood guard on
the top of the escarpment. In the British Museum there
is an altar discovered during the excavations of the
Roman fort at Lympne in 1850. A worn inscription tells

Lympne Castle, Hythe

us that 'Aufidius Pantera, Praefect of the British Fleet' had dedicated it to some diety, probably Neptune. Professor Haverfield suggests that the altar was erected in the 2nd century, in which case Portus Lemanus, a natural harbour of great importance to the Romans was possibly the port upon which the fleet was based.

The site of the harbour was almost certainly where Lympne crosses the Royal Military Canal south of Lympne Castle. The road down the hill is on the line of the Roman road from Canterbury to Portus Lemanus. This ties in with the ruins of Stutfall Castle, one of the Saxon Shore forts which has virtually disappeared. Excavations have revealed that it covered roughly ten acres with walls twenty feet in height and twelve feet thick. It would be safe to assume, therefore, that it was very similar to Pevensey and with a similar entrance gateway. Landslides and the poaching of stones wanted for building have left archaeologists very little on which to work, but there is enough evidence to tell us something about the size and importance of the place.

St. Stephen's Church, Lympne, built by Lanfranc, first Norman Archbishop of Canterbury

Lympne Castle is now the property of descendants of the famous painter Benjamin West. The cabinet where the artist stored his sketches stands in the Great Hall of the castle and on it are the Wedgwood pigment pots in which he mixed his paints.

The castle is reputed to be haunted! There is the ghost of the Roman soldier who walks the eastern tower on the site of the Roman look-out. No doubt he continues to keep watch and ward so that we may have adequate warning when an enemy is seen. There is also the ghost of a Saxon priest, one of seven who lived here after the Conquest. All seven, it is said, were murdered by the Normans. The Domesday Book provides proof of their existence, for they are duly recorded, but there is no evidence as to what happened to them.

Close to the castle, almost adjoining, in fact, is the Norman church of St. Stephen. It is the work of Lanfranc, much altered and restored. Lanfranc was also responsible for the original conversion into an archdeacons' residence of what was once a Saxon Abbey. The church, commanding a superb view over the marsh was undoubtedly a hide-out for smugglers, and from it the approach of Revenue men could be signalled to smugglers on the beach below. A few years ago an old square pew was removed from the chancel and beneath its floor the workmen found a chamber large enough to conceal an entire cargo.

Flowing through Hythe is the Royal Military Canal, which runs from Cliff End at Hastings to Hythe. To look on it now, with its gay dinghies, and the trees lining the banks it is hard to realise the canal was never cut as a commercial enterprise and would, in fact, serve no commercial end. It was created at the insistence of William Pitt, Warden of the Cinque Ports from 1792 as one of the defences against the threat of invasion from France. It is not by any means a conventional canal, but is constructed with abrupt bends at strategic points where guns

St. Stephen's Church, Lympne, the interior

can be brought to bear along the line of the waterway itself in order to enfilade the attacking forces.

The Martello towers which were coincident with the canal were developed as the almost direct result of an attempt by British naval units to blockade certain Corsican ports and to secure a base for future operations. To do this, the capture of a tower on Mortella Point at the entrance to San Fiorenza Bay was vital. Two attacks were made, the first by the frigate HMS *Lowestoft,* the second by a 74-gun ship, the *Fortitude* assisted by the 32-gun sloop *Juno.* Both attacks ended in failure, the ships being forced to withdraw with heavy casualties and damage.

The result of these engagements was to underline a lesson that might have been learned earlier had Henry VIII's 'Tudor Rose' castles been attacked, namely, that a shore-based fixed-gun platform could inflict terrible damage upon an enemy attempting a seaborne landing.

British military engineers seized upon the idea and the first 'Martello' towers were built in 1796. The name given to these squat little forts is a corruption of the name of the tower on Mortella Point, due it is said, to a spelling error on the part of a ships' writer. In all 194 towers were built, including some on the Suffolk coast. The idea caught on. Two towers were built in South Africa, more in North America and Nova Scotia and a few in Ireland. They were circular in design, the average height being around forty feet with a base diameter of forty-five feet and walls fifteen feet thick. The door was set high and could only be reached by a scaling ladder, to guard against surprise. Virtually impregnable they were built of brick set in lime, ash and hot tallow, which cooled to the hardness of iron, so that cannon balls simply bounced off. The armament consisted of a 24-pounder long gun on a traversing slide, with two $5\frac{1}{2}$-inch howitzers. Each tower cost £3,000.

There is an interesting little church at Stone on the

fringe of the marsh. It contains a stone which bears the weathered outline of a bull. This has led to the belief that it is part of an altar dedicated to the Roman god Mithras. In the past it was not considered suitable for a Christian church and was used for some time as a horse block at the Black Ox Inn, from where it was rescued by the Reverend William Guestling, for whose father Purcell wrote the anthem '*They that go down to the sea in ships*'. Near it are the fossilised bones of an iguanodon excavated at a local quarry in 1935.

Not far away is Smallhythe, the port for Tenterden, which, as a Corporate Member of Rye was entitled to Cinque Ports privileges. Henry VIII visited Smallhythe to inspect the progress in the building of a warship for the Royal fleet, but today, instead of a thriving little port there are only green fields and woods, so that it is hard to believe that the place ever boasted a dockyard and quays.

Appledore, the Royal Military Canal

New Romney, Lydd, and Dymchurch

Situated almost exactly midway between the Kent and Sussex ports, Romney exercised a special role in the Confederation, for it was so obviously the most suitable place for meetings of the Brodhull and Guestling. It was for this reason that Romney became the custodian of the Cinque Ports records, as well as those of the town, which dates from the 14th century. It was here that the historic Black and White Books were stored as well as the Bailiff's records of the Yarmouth Herring Fair. The White Book contains the minutes of the meetings of the Brodhull from 1433 to 1571 and the Black Book those of the combined courts of Brodhull and Guestling from 1572. Frequent references to these records are contained in the text of this book, and anyone wishing to study the history of the Confederation owes a debt of gratitude to Dr. Felix Hull, of Maidstone, for undertaking the task of indexing and classification.

Romney once stood at the mouth of the Rother but the Great Storm of 1287 caused the river to silt up, after which, deprived of its natural outlet the Rother changed its course! Almost overnight Romney's status as a port was lost and today there is no trace of the bay which once provided a sheltered anchorage for ships.

Largely as a result 'New Romney' came into being in the first half of the 13th century. The term 'new' is, therefore, strictly relative but the distinction is an important one. New Romney is a Cinque Port, with all the special status and privileges of a Cinque Port, which probably accounts for a great deal of the friction which in the past existed between the Barons of the Cinque Ports and the Marshmen.

New Romney is the traditional home of the mystery play, and strolling players from there travelled to the most remote of the marsh towns and villages, an enterprise not to be lightly undertaken at a time when roads were virtually non-existent and footpads plentiful. A gibe frequently directed at Kent and Sussex was that their womenfolk had longer legs than most because they were forever pulling their feet out of the marsh mud!

Romney Marsh is famous for its churches, but of the five listed in Domesday only one survives—that of St. Nicholas in New Romney. It has a magnificent Norman tower, and some idea of the antiquity of the fabric can be gleaned from the marks inside the church showing how high the 13th-century floodwaters rose. The fact that the West doorway is below the present ground level is due, it is said to the mass of mud and shingle deposited during the Great Storm.

The church was used from ancient times for Cinque Ports meetings and it was around the tomb of Richard Stuppenye in the south aisle that the Jurats assembled each year to elect the mayor. This practice continued without a break until the use of churches for such purposes was barred by an Act of Parliament in the 19th century.

The contrast between New and Old Romney is quite startling. With its ancient church dedicated to St. Clement, Old Romney is a tranquil refuge in which it is difficult to believe in the bustling activities of long ago. The church is really old, its nave constructed in the very early days of the Conquest. The font, which dates to about 1300 rests on four pillars each of which has a completely different capital. In one of the best church guides to be found anywhere in South-East England, Miss Anne Roper has described the badly worn figures on the capitals as a tiny man with his hands on his knees, another with his fingers in his mouth, a third with the face of a monkey and the fourth is a priest. There does not appear to be a logical explanation for these figures.

*　　*　　*

Lydd, which gave the explosive 'lyddite' its name, has a character all its own. Looking at the nuclear power

West Door, St. Nicholas' Church, New Romney

station at Dungeness it is far from easy to picture it as an island, when it possessed a harbour, yet there is an air of something not easily defined about the place, as if it were saying that neither nuclear power stations nor artillery ranges have the means of disturbing this splendid isolation. The peaceful oasis around the church seems to offer a refuge from the noise and confusion of the modern world so that when it is time to go, one experiences a queer reluctance to take the first step.

The pride of Lydd lies in its church, which is of noble proportions. The tower rises to over 130 feet. Cardinal Wolsey raised it when Rector of Lydd. In the north chapel a visitor will find the tomb of Clement Stuppenye, great grandson of Richard Stuppenye, of New Romney. The tomb here served the same purpose as that in the Church of St. Nicholas at New Romney when the commonalty would assemble round it for the election of the Jurats. The church was very badly damaged during the last war—amongst other things the chancel was completely destroyed—but it has been beautifully restored with all the original beauty retained.

The man who saw Captain Cook clubbed to death in the South Pacific and who subsequently gave evidence at the Naval enquiry which followed lies in Lydd Church-yard. He was Lieutenant Thomas Edgar, and his grave is marked by a large tombstone on which the following epitaph can be made out:

> Tom Edgar at last has sailed out of this world,
> His shroud is put on; his tops'ls are furled.
> He lies snug in Death's boat,
> Without any concern
> And is moored for a full due ahead and astern.
> O'er the compass of life he has merrily run,
> His voyage is completed, his reckoning is done.

*　　*　　*

St. Mary's-in-the-Marsh, Romney Marsh

'It was Russell Thorndyke who really put Dymchurch on the map,' said an acquaintance. 'Thousands of people who would never have heard of the place in the ordinary way know all about Dr. Syn!'

The fact that Dymchurch is the seat of government of the Marsh is of relatively little importance compared with the fictional exploits of the smuggling parson!

Romney Marsh, which extends from Hythe in the east to the Sussex boundary line in the west is roughly twelve miles across. The greater part of it would be under water today but for the great sea wall built at Dymchurch, which is four miles long. It is a massive structure by any standard, more than twenty feet high and from fifteen to thirty feet wide. It is faced on the seaward side by blocks of stone, with groynes every few yards, and pierced in three places with sluices to regulate the draining of the marsh. The importance of the wall can be estimated if one walks along the road on the landward side at high tide, for then the sea beating against its southern slope is above one's head!

80

CHAPTER VI

The Ports of Rye and Winchelsea

Described in various charters and records as the 'Antient Towns' Rye and Winchelsea acquired their status as quasi-head ports in the Charter of 1278, which was unusual as embracing the five ports and the two 'antient' towns jointly. At that time they fulfilled a role which made them important members of the Confederation, but their history goes much further back. It goes back to the days when the Romans made use of the forest ridge running through Battle to Netherfield and Uckfield as the most direct route for the movement of iron recovered at Battle and Sedlescombe.

Later, Rye and Winchelsea were contained in the manors of Ramslie and Brede, promised by Ethelred the Unready to the Abbots of Fécamp. Ethelred died in 1016 before his intentions could be put into effect, and his heir, Edmund Ironside, did nothing to honour his father's wishes, his brief but ineffective campaign against the Danes probably occupying his whole attention.

Ironically enough, it was Canute, who had married Queen Emma, Ethelred's widow, who, when he became King, finally ratified the grant of the two manors and in so doing, repaid the abbots for giving aid and sanctuary to his mortal enemy!

The twin towns thus came under monastic control, a state of affairs which continued until the reign of Henry III when, in 1247, both towns became Crown property. In exchange Fécamp was given the manor of Cheltenham. During this period changes were taking place in the coastline, but while silting up and the accumulation of great masses of shingle continued to alter the character of a number of ports, Rye escaped serious damage, though part of the lower town was inundated in 1340. As previously noted, the Great Storm of 1287 which completely destroyed the old Winchelsea and crippled Romney actually benefited Rye by changing the course of the Rother, causing it to empty itself into the sea.

There had been previous storms violent enough to be recorded but it was the final tempest of 1287 which completed the destruction of Winchelsea both as a port and as a town. Owing to its vulnerability, as opposed to Rye safely perched on its hilltop, a commission ordered by Edward I to report on the matter, recommended the abandonment of the existing town and its re-siting on higher ground. The site selected was on the heights of Iham, where the present town stands. The wine trade with Gascony was regarded as of primary importance at that time and even now beautifully constructed wine

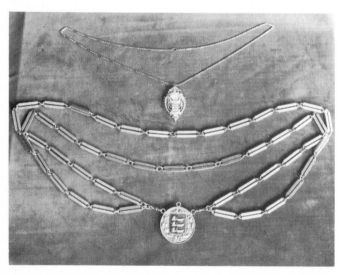

Mayoral Insignia, Rye, showing the Arms of the Cinque Ports

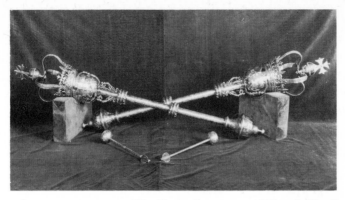

The Maces, Rye   [*Photo J. Wood*]

cellars survive under many of the houses. The new town is a classic example of medieval town planning. Instead of a haphazard huddle of cottages around a church it is developed on a grid-iron 'bastide' pattern of straight roads criss-crossing at regular intervals and so providing the plots of land allocated for dwelling and business premises.

The site of the great church of St. Thomas the Martyr was selected so that it formed the centre point of the new town. Town walls were built and the harbour developed where the River Brede flows past the northern end of the peninsula. According to a survey of 1291 the annual rent for the 800 plots which comprised the town was £14 11s. 5¾d. These rents are still collected by the Town Chamberlain but they now go to the town instead of to the Crown.

Rye, on the other hand, retains much of its medieval charm, despite being the victim of many ferocious raids by the French. These began about 1330 and reached some kind of a climax when, in 1339 Winchelsea was attacked and over a hundred houses were burned. Again in 1359 a force of over three thousand French landed at Winchelsea and attacked the town while the townspeople were crowded in the church of St. Giles (of which there is no trace today). According to Thomas of Walsingham such scenes of rape and slaughter took place as had never before been witnessed. Henry of Knighton testified that there were nine illustrious women ravished and forty townsmen killed and that the French sailed away a day later with thirteen ships loaded with wine and victuals.

The lane where the dead bodies lay before burial is still known as Dead Man's Lane.

Rye had its share of slaughter as well. In 1377 a particularly ferocious raid left the town a smouldering ruin. In this instance Winchelsea was saved by the Abbot of Battle who brought a force of men-at-arms to the rescue. In the following year the men of Rye and Winchelsea combined in a joint retaliatory raid in which the church bells of Rye, stolen by the French the year before, were retrieved and triumphantly restored to their rightful place.

With the end of the Hundred Years War Rye entered upon a period of comparative prosperity, and by the middle of the 15th century could claim to have one of the most important of the Cinque Ports harbours, though even then the sea was beginning to retreat. Like Sandwich, Rye gave asylum to the Huguenots who fled across the Channel after the massacre of St. Bartholomew's Day, bringing with them their skills and crafts. Cloth and paper making became industries in their own right and such was the impact of this influx of foreigners that many families in the twin towns can today trace their French origin in their surnames.

Queen Elizabeth visited Rye in 1573 and named the town Rye Royal. If this gives Rye a special status, Winchelsea can claim to have witnessed the birth of Methodism, for in 1773 John Wesley came to Winchelsea and opened a little chapel in which, today, can be found the pulpit from which he preached. It was to Winchelsea that he returned in 1790 to preach his last open air sermon under a large tree beside the church a few nights before

84

he died. The spot is marked for the visitor by a notice at the foot of an ash tree which replaced the original one, blown down in a storm.

The church of St. Thomas the Martyr is partly a ruin, but from what is left it is possible to imagine the splendour of the great building when it was first dedicated. The oak timbers of the roof came from the great forest of Anderida, while Caen stone was brought from Normandy. In the Allard Chantry is the tomb of Gervase Allard, Admiral of the Fleet and the first Portsman to have borne the title of Admiral of the Cinque Ports. The painting by Millais called 'The Random Shot' portrays a child, covered by a soldier's cloak, asleep on the tomb. The original is in the Sheffield Collection. Among the foliage of the tomb's canopy can be seen the carved heads of Edward I and his second Queen, Margaret of France.

The Town Well is in Castle Street, housed in a small building in which is a notice informing all and sundry that the well is closed at seven o'clock at night and

Rye, old houses by the churchyard

Ypres Tower, Rye

opened at six o'clock in the morning and is closed all day on the Sabbath. Near it is the Court Hall, part of which goes back to the 13th century. Here the Jurats and Councillors held their meetings and every Easter Monday the new mayor is elected in the Upper Hall. For a long time the town prison was on the ground floor.

Tradition dies hard in Winchelsea, which is probably the reason why the self-perpetuating system of electing the town's Freemen, who in turn elect the mayor, has lasted for close on seven hundred years. As a thoroughly undemocratic 'closed shop' the arrangement must be unique, for each Freeman is elected for life! But it works!

There are the remains of a Franciscan Friary not far from the church. Part of the Chapel of the Virgin Mary remains but little else. Built in 1300 it was dissolved at the time of the Reformation. It is said that Thackery was inspired to write his unfinished novel *Denis Duval* by the activities of the Weston brothers, who lived in Winchelsea without anyone suspecting the source of their apparent wealth. Until, that is, they were caught robbing the Bristol mail!

Today, Winchelsea remains aloof, far removed from the bustle of commercial life—a town in a trance, as Coventry Patmore described it. Only in Winchelsea would you find a keeper of The Lookout employed for a weekly wage for $5\frac{1}{2}$d. (2p) to watch for the ships of likely invaders, an appointment only terminated in 1970!

But then, why not? After all, the newly elected mayor of its twin town, Rye, throws showers of hot pennies from the steps of the Town Hall, a custom much appreciated by the children of the town!

Hastings

In the 12th century Hastings was contributing twenty ships to the royal fleet but with the silting up of the harbour and by the time of the great storm of 1287 the town was already much reduced in status and power. By

Rye, Mermaid Street

St. Mary the Virgin, Rye

Tomb of Gervase Allard, first Admiral of the Cinque Ports

the middle of the 13th century it was supplying only six ships while Rye and Winchelsea were contributing fifteen between them. As in the case of Romney and Sandwich the Portsmen did not tamely accept a state of affairs that was quite obviously going to reduce the once prosperous and important port to the level of a mere fishing village, but despite all their efforts to build a new harbour they were fighting against forces too big for them. The last attempt was in the late 19th century but the sea once again proved victorious, the broken western arm of the projected breakwater being now all that remains to underline the futility of trying to achieve the impossible.

The role of Hastings in our island story was equal to that of any of the ports, nevertheless. It was from Hastings that King John, in 1201, proclaimed British Sovereignty of the Seas, while, dominating the town from its eminence on the cliff top, are the ruins of the great castle built soon after the Conquest, replacing the temporary strong point depicted in the Bayeaux Tapestry. Just for the record it should be pointed out that the Bayeaux Tapestry is not a tapestry at all but an embroidery! It has been called the Bayeux Tapestry for so long that it is doubtful if it would be recognised by another name.

Near the castle are the remains of St. Mary's Collegiate Church, of which Thomas à Becket was once the Dean. It was here that Anselm preached to King Stephen and here Alice, Countess of Eu worshipped, and pilgrims came to their journey's end at the chapel of the Holy Cross. Attached to the church was a grammar school and a sing-ing school, but it is a very long time since the voices of the choir mingled with the mewing of the gulls flying in-land before the threat of a coming storm. Close by are the so-called Smugglers' Caves, a maze of underground pas-sages created by flood water centuries ago and now a place where tourists step for a brief moment into a vanished past.

The two oldest churches in Hastings are St. Clements and All Saints. St. Clements was razed by the French in 1377 and rebuilt in 1390. Later, near the end of the 17th century a passing French ship fired a broad-side into the town, one of the cannon balls lodging near the top of the tower. The townspeople left it there and placed another near it as a gesture of defiance! Dante Gabriel Rosetti was married to Elizabeth Siddal in St. Clements in 1860. Ill and disillusioned, Elizabeth died of an overdose of laudanum in 1862.

All Saints was rebuilt in 1436. The father of Titus Oates was a former Rector and Titus himself was baptised in the church at the age of eleven. Expelled from school, sent down from university he became curate of All Saints where, it is said, his conduct was such that the congrega-tion threw him out.

Hastings had two Corporate Members of the Confeder-ation after Rye and Winchelsea acquired Head Port status.

These were Seaford and Pevensey. Seaford was an important medieval town, with a good harbour at the mouth of the Ouse, but the course of the river was changed in 1579, the harbour silted up, and today there is no trace of what was evidently once a busy and thriving port. The church of St. Leonard has two very early Norman windows in the tower, and one of the piers has a gallery of figures showing the stoning of Stephen, the Baptism of Christ, Peter with his Key and John the Baptist. Above these is a crude sculpture of St. George killing the dragon.

Pevensey, like so many of the Cinque Ports has been left high and dry by the receding sea, so that the historic landing place of William the Conqueror has gone. All we have left are the encircling walls of the Saxon-Shore fort which has already been described, and enclosed within them the Norman castle built by Robert of Mortain, half-brother to the Conqueror.

The castle has a long and colourful history, for it became the custom to grant the honour of Pevensey

Remains of ancient Church of St. Thomas the Martyr, Winchelsea

91

Hastings, the old town

A part of the old town, Hastings

to the Queens of England. Thus Margaret, second wife of Edward I and Phillipa, Queen of Edward III were responsible for appointing Constables. In 1372 the honour was given to John of Gaunt, whose son Henry claimed the crown as Henry IV in 1399. As a result Pevensey was besieged by the forces of Richard II, for the Constable, Sir John Pelham, had thrown in his lot with the usurper. The castle was held for him by Lady Joan Pelham, whose letter to her husband is probably one of the earliest written by a lady of quality in English. From the wording it can be assumed that Sir John had succeeded in getting a letter smuggled into the castle. Lady Joan's reply is a masterpiece of understatement.

She wrote:

I recommend me to your lordship with heart and body and with all my poor might and with all this I thank you as my dearest and best loved of all earthly lords.

By my troth I was never so glad as when I heard ye were strong enough with the grace of God to keep ye from the malice of your enemies. And, my dear lord, if it like you to know my fare I am here laid by in the manner of a siege with the county of Sussex, Surrey and a large parcel of Kent so that I may not go out nor no victuals get me!

Farewell, my dear lord, the Holy Trinity keep you from your enemies and soon send me good tidings of you. Written at Pevensey in the castle by your own poor
J. Pelham.

With the threat of German invasion in 1940 Pevensey Castle once again became a strategic strong point in our coastal defences. It was refortified as a command post and was in continuous military occupation until 1944. The defence works were carefully camouflaged to look like the original ruin. Shards of Roman pottery found where the sea once washed against the south-eastern outer walls, together with bricks stamped **HON AVG ANDRIA** and which clearly refer to Honorius (395–423) indicate a time span of over fifteen hundred years during which Pevensey was a link in the long chain of fortifications guarding our shores. A long, long, time by any standard!

Seaford

Originally a Saxon town, Seaford rested at the mouth of the Ouse, which was tidal as far as Lewes. There are traces of a prehistoric camp or hill fort on Seaford Head, dating to approximately 300 BC. The cliffs stand three hundred feet above sea level at this point, and afford a magnificent view all around. From the fact that a Roman cemetery lies a little to the north it would seem that the Romans occupied the site at some time.

The parish church is dedicated to St. Leonard. It was built by the Normans in 1080. Although at one time it had fallen almost into ruin and was later restored, two of the original nave windows can be seen above the two

St. Clement's Church, Hastings

St. Clement's Church, Hastings, showing two cannon balls on each
side of the window

arches which were built in 1120. One of the Norman piers has a gallery of figures showing the stoning of Stephen, the Baptism of Christ, Peter and his Key and John the Baptist.

The decline of Seaford as a port for Lewes was accelerated in the 16th century when the Ouse changed its course and a new harbour was built at Newhaven. Once notorious for its wreckers, the town gained an unenviable reputation during the lean years of the 17th and 18th centuries, when the population dramatically declined. Even as late as 1809, when six ships were wrecked in Seaford Bay, the looting of the cargoes was described by a contemporary writer as 'a disgrace to Englishmen'. There is a figurehead outside the Star Inn in Alfriston which came from a ship wrecked at Seaford and looted three hundred years ago.

On the credit side of the ledger Seaford can claim the honour of being the birthplace of Rosalie Harvey, the daughter of the vicar in the mid-19th century. At the age of twenty-eight she went to India with the Zenana Mission to Poona from where, later on she moved to Nasik, where she worked for the rest of her life.

For fifty years she laboured in her own particular vineyard, creating her famous Babies' Homes for homeless children. But of all her achievements her work among the lepers ranks highest. During a period of famine when she worked in a relief camp she came across such terrible cases of leprosy that she started her first leper asylum in an iron hut which barely held the beds she bought with the meagre funds at her disposal. She was given the Kaisar-i-Hind medal but her real monument was the work she did, the love she inspired. When she died she had the comfort of knowing that thousands she had rescued from want, misery and despair were leading useful and rewarding lives and that, whatever else might happen, her work would go on.

With the Conquest an accomplished fact, Sussex was

divided into *rapes*, each rape having a castle, a river and a port. As we have noted, the lordship of the rape of Pevensey was granted to Robert of Mortain, the Conqueror's half brother; that of Lewes was given to William de Warenne, husband of Gundrada, reputed daughter of the Conqueror. Although not a member of the Confederation, Lewes was nevertheless closely linked with Seaford, not only as the county town but also by virtue of the Ouse being navigable as far upstream as Lewes. In the early 15th century we have a record by the Bailiff describing twelve sail moored to the wharves in Lewes.

The castle dates from the early days of the Conquest and is remarkable for possessing two *mottes*, or artificial mounds and provides an early example of the use of stone fortifications in the shell keep on the western mound.

Below the castle, and close to the river are the remains of the once great Priory of St. Pancras, a Clunic establishment built on the site of a Saxon church. The manor of St. Pancras was given to the Abbots of Cluny by Gundrada in return for their help when, on a pilgrimage

Pevensey, curtain wall and barbican tower

Pevensey, Oubliette

to Rome, she and her husband were taken ill. On their deaths, William and Gundrada were buried in lead cysts below the High Altar of the Priory Church, but when the Priory was destroyed during the Reformation it was found they had been spirited away. They were discovered by workmen building the Lewes to Brighton railway line, and after a careful and scientific identification were re-interred in what has come to be called Gundrada's Chapel, in the church of St. John in Southover.

After the Conquest the new lords of Lewes found it necessary to exercise suzerainty over the district but later the chief citizens were organised into a Merchant's Guild, their rights embodied in a charter of Reginald de Warenne in the reign of King Stephen. William de Warenne, grandson of the Conqueror's companion was absent on a Crusade at the time and Reginald, his brother, was acting in his place. William's death at the hands of the Moslems in 1147 gives us an approximate date for the charter, which reads:

99

Reginald de Warenne to the Sheriff of Lewes and to all Barons of the Earl and to the rest of his men as well French and English, Greeting! Know ye that by the Common Council of the Prior of St. Pancras and the Barons of the Earl I have restored to the Burgesses of Lewes a Merchant Gild with all the customs and dignities which belong to the same as freely and quietly as they had the same in the time of my grandfather and of my father for twenty shillings to be paid yearly to the provostry of Lewes and subject to this Agreement that if my brother the Earl shall withdraw the Grant I will urge my best endeavours that he shall grant to them the aforesaid Gild for the same annual rent but if not I engage as far as I can that my Lord William the King's son shall grant them the same.

This historic document is probably one of the earliest of its kind and is remarkable for the wording, implicit as it is with that sense of responsibility to their people which marked the de Warenne family.

Pevensey, remains of the Keep.

Pevensey, walls and bastion of later Norman Castle

One of the most important events in the history of Lewes, however, was the battle fought on the slopes of the downs to the west of the town between the forces of Henry III and Simon de Montfort. As a result of the defeat of the king's army the Mise of Lewes was signed, a document which ushered Parliamentary government into England for the first time. The round house at the end of Pipe's Passage was once the base of the windmill which supplied the castle with water and it was here that the King took refuge after the battle.

In its long and colourful history probably nothing has made a greater impact on the ordinary men and women of the town than the Marian persecution of the Protestants. The Lewes Martyrs whose memorial, oddly enough, stands on a high hill far from the scene of their immolation, numbered seventeen. Simple people with a simple faith and a belief in the justice and mercy of God, they choose death in its most horrible form rather than depart from those beliefs and principles by which they had been

Lewes, Anne of Cleves' House

Lewes, notice in Keere St.

brought up. Their memories are hallowed in Lewes even to this day.

The ancient records of the town contain much to interest the historian. We read of the munitions sent from Lewes 'in the time that the Spanyshe fleet came along by New Haven'. After the danger of 1588 had passed we learn of the two barrels of powder of which one was '*by the holl consent of the fellowship spent in shooting off the Great Pieces of the Castle att the Rejoysing days for the overthrow of the Spanyshe fleet, commanded by the Council*'.

Lewes has produced many famous people during its long history, including the great physician and geologist Dr. Gideon Mantell, who practised at Castle Place. The diarist, Evelyn, attended the Old Grammar School, and from the Springette family, long seated at Ringmer, William Penn took his wife.

Today the steep and winding High Street retains much of the atmosphere of its past, but it remains for the Council notice at the foot of Keere Street, a steep and narrow roadway leading from the High Street to the Market Place to remind us that times have indeed changed, but whether for better or for worse, who can say?

The notice reads:

KEERE STREET.
NO THROUGH ROAD.

Although recorded in history that George IV, when Prince Regent, once drove a coach and four down Keere Street for a wager, access by vehicles to and from the High Street is now forbidden.

By Order.
Borough of Lewes.

CHAPTER VII

Press Gangs and Smugglers

The creation of a professional navy in the 16th century accelerated the decline in importance of the Cinque Ports, but not of the Portsmen themselves. Seamen born and bred, they were the type the navy needed and needed badly, but the appalling conditions of life on a King's ship, the poor pay, bad food and savage discipline were not such as to induce men who valued their liberty and independence above all else, to volunteer.

And so the Press Gang was born.

Today we can only marvel at a state of affairs which allowed such things to happen. There was no discrimination, nor were there any means by which a pressed man could appeal against his cruel fate. Seized in the street or while drinking in some waterfront tavern, any attempt at resistance was summarily dealt with, a broken skull being more often than not, the reward for putting up a fight. Once on board the ship to which they were taken the wretched victims of this brutal method of recruitment had The Articles of War read to them, whether they were conscious or not, and from that moment they were, willy nilly, in the King's pay. That meant that even a hint of insubordination was punishable by flogging or, in extreme cases, by death. No provision of any kind was made for a man's wife and family, and more often than not, only his failure to return home gave a hint as to his probable fate.

Men, aided and abetted by their womenfolk, went to the most extraordinary lengths to avoid impressment and lookouts were posted to give warning when the Press gang

Lewes, the Barbican

was about. This usually consisted of a dozen or more hand picked bullies under an officer, and it was a case of woe betide them, if they returned to their ship without the required quota. It was not a matter of wonder, therefore, that the mere sight of a King's ship off one of the Ports was enough to send most of the able-bodied fishermen into hiding.

Hiding from the Press gangs was not difficult for men who knew every shaw and coombe in the fertile coastal plain, every devious twisting track across the marshes and who could count upon every man and woman they might meet as an ally. Nor could the Press gangs hope to follow. There was no time, for one thing and, for another, it was far too dangerous! Their chief and possibly their only advantage was surprise—the sudden onset in a crowded smoky tavern with men posted at doors and windows to see that none escaped.

To accuse the Portsmen of being dyed in the wool law-breakers would be an over simplification, as it would be to describe them as pirates first and fishermen afterwards. There was a very fine line drawn between piracy and privateering in the days when the King did not hesitate to make use of the latter, and much the same could be said about smuggling. A man who had been forced to go into hiding for a time at least, would have no qualms about joining one of the numerous gangs of smugglers 'working' the coast.

There were two main groups, the 'owlers' whose name came from the signal they used, which was the call of the owl, and the so-called 'freetraders' of the 18th and 19th centuries. The owlers were the professionals, tough, resourceful and with no loyalties save to one another. They had their origin in medieval times when a heavy tax was levied on wool exported to the Continent. Wool was then the basis of the national economy and it was a product for which there was an ever increasing demand. The risks were great but then so was the profit.

The 'freetraders' for the most part, were Portsmen who ran a profitable sideline in smuggled brandy, wine and tobacco. There were few who were not involved in this trade in some way or another, and while we have seen that Dr. Syn was a figment of a writer's imagination, his counterparts in both Kent and Sussex undoubtedly existed.

In the 18th and 19th centuries smuggling in Kent and Sussex assumed gigantic proportions. The narrow waters of the Channel lent themselves to fast and comparatively easy crossings when conditions were favourable, and the smugglers had a wide choice of suitable landing places created by the variation in the character of the coast itself. Marshland between Rye and Hythe gives place to the vast expanse of shingle at Dungeness, while the North Downs, terminating at Folkestone, form the base of the high cliff line extending to Dover. The Isle of Thanet, separated from the dip slope of the downs by the Wantsum Channel provided something in the nature of a smugglers paradise, where Preventive officers and men could and did flounder

Lewes, Old houses in Keere St.

from one muddy creek to another without even catching a glimpse of their quarry.

The Navy was powerless to help. Undermined and badly equipped it was already fully extended. Britain had been forced out of the Mediterranean and we were left without an ally in Europe, while the Dutch fleet at Texel threatened the East Coast. The mutinies at Spithead and the Nore underlined the bankruptcy of a policy that had nothing to commend it. The brutality and floggings in both Army and Navy had shocked even the case-hardened Prussians. The pay was poor and always overdue, the food rotten while the contractors and ships' chandlers grew rich on illicit profits and speculation. Commissions were bought and sold so that promotion scarcely ever went by merit and when the press gangs failed to produce the required number of 'recruits' the gaols were opened in order to swell the total.

Just before the Nore and Spithead mutinies news was circulated along the south east coast that thirteen men of the Oxford Militia were to be tried for mutiny at Brighton. Part of a force stationed at East Blatchington on the outskirts of Seaford, they had rebelled in protest at the small quantity and poor quality of their rations. They broke into a flour mill and tipped the cargo of a vessel loaded with grain into the Ouse at Newhaven.

Brighton at that time was the military headquarters of the force poised to repel a possible French invasion, so the men were tried by court martial in the Castle Tavern close to what is now Castle Square. Two of the ringleaders, Henry Parrish and Edward Cooke were sentenced to be shot and six others to receive one thousand lashes, tantamount to being flogged to death.

The savage sentences sent a wave of horror through the town and a number of influential residents got up petitions begging for mercy for the condemned men, but without result. The sentences were carried out at Goldstone Bottom, where the Brighton and Hove Albion football ground now stands, Cooke and Parrish kneeling on their coffins. Those sentenced to be flogged were cut free after receiving three hundred lashes each, the army surgeon in charge protesting they could stand no more. The chaplain of the Regiment, the Rev. M. Dring fainted when the fatal volleys were fired and, it is said, never afterwards wholly recovered his mind.

At this time the entire financial structure of the nation seemed on the verge of collapse. Prices soared astronomically, and there was a great deal of actual starvation amongst the poor.

Despite Nelson and the gradual return to a position where sea power counted, there remained one serious threat to the chances of recovery. This was the league of Northern powers called The Armed Neutrality which was designed to prevent, by force of arms if need be, the search of their vessels by British ships, for contraband. This worked in favour of the smugglers, as can be seen from the affair of the lugger *Four Brothers*, a Folkestone boat which carried a crew of twenty-six, most of them from Folkestone. The smugglers were intercepted on the way from Flushing with over a hundred tons of leaf tobacco on board, together with a small quantity of brandy and tea. Off Dieppe His Majesty's Revenue Cutter *Badger*, commanded by Lieutenant Nazer came up with the lugger and ordered her to heave-to.

The *Four Brothers*, which was armed with four small carronades, immediately opened fire, wounding the commander of the *Badger* and killing one of the crew. In the fight which followed, one of the crew of the *Four Brothers* was also killed and the lugger dismasted. The *Four Brothers* was taken into Dover and the captain and the crew were housed on board a frigate, in irons. Three of the wounded died there.

At the trial, which took place in London twenty-two of the lugger's crew faced the court. They were charged with feloniously and with malice aforethought firing upon

Canterbury Cathedral

the revenue cutter *Badger* and killing one of the crew. For the defence it was contended that the *Four Brothers* was a Dutch ship and that the crew all had Dutch names! The trial judge, Mr. Justice Park instructed the jury that if no part of the lugger belonged to any British subject and if one half of the crew were not His Majesty's subjects then the *Badger* had no right to open fire. Needless to say the jury brought in a verdict of 'Not Guilty' and the *Four Brothers* returned to Folkestone with its cargo still intact!

Other affrays took place, for this was a period in which the power of the smugglers and the rich rewards to be collected from the sale of goods in the black market justified almost any risk. Cargoes were run nightly and reports in the *Cinque Ports Herald* often referred to pitched battles between smugglers and Revenue men at Camber and on the marshes. The Rev. Richard Harris Barham, author of the Ingoldsby Legends, records meeting smugglers at night as he rode from Snargate to Warehorne. He was allowed to continue on his way and as he

Canterbury, the West Door

did so a large and strangely silent company would file past, each man leading a horse on which kegs were slung.

It was in the reign of Edward III that the 'tunnage and poundage' levy was introduced to provide money for what was called The Keeping of the Seas. Two shillings a tun was levied on all wine imports in addition to a two and a half per cent duty on all imports except wine. The exactions of the customs, which grew in pace with the growth of the national debt became, in the reign of William III a burden so crushing that it elevated the smuggling of foreign goods from a sideline to a major industry.

It is interesting to note that here, when Kent and Sussex smugglers *were* apprehended they frequently advanced the argument that, as the Cinque Ports had been 'quit of prisage time out of mind' they were doing no wrong! In bringing foreign goods into the country without paying dues they were, they claimed, merely exercising their ancient and long established rights. The authorities remained unconvinced and the war between the Preventive men and the freetraders continued. Volumes could be written about the ingenious devices and subterfuges invented to fool the authorities but it remains a fact that the failure to put down smuggling at a time when it was making serious inroads into the national purse was due very largely to a combination of circumstances almost impossible to combat.

Firstly, the smugglers were men of undoubted courage and were possessed of a high degree of technical skill. They were men who boasted they could outsail and out manoeuvre any revenue cutter launched. They had the backing of those who provided the means by which fast, armed luggers built at Rye and Hastings were readily obtainable as well as the connivance of the local gentry. Innkeeper, harbour master, parson or squire, it made no real difference. All participated in one way or another, from passing on information to hiding a cargo landed secretly in some hidden cove on a dark, moonless night.

Roman trench system, Richborough

Secondly, it must be remembered that an army, and a large one at that, would have been required to cover all the landing places to be found between Selsey Bill and Dover. As it was, patrols were woefully inadequate and hopelessly outnumbered. One result was that the luggers made what amounted to scheduled runs to and from the various ports on the French coast. Sloops and frigates which could have been used close inshore and were fast enough were fully engaged in the blockade of the enemy ports. This left the pitifully few Revenue cutters to cope as best they might, outwitted at every turn by an enterprising foe who, it seemed, knew in advance every move the luckless Preventive officers might make.

Inevitably, of course, the hard liners among the smugglers became organised into gangs. These became notorious in Kent and Sussex and, realising their lives were forfeit if caught, their members developed into criminals of a most vicious type.

114

It follows that the profits were great. When tea could be bought on the Continent for sevenpence a pound it fetched five shillings in London, and brandy, bought in France for £1 for a four gallon keg retailed at five times that price on the black market. A Rye-built lugger could easily carry from eighty to ninety kegs as well as other commodities.

Apart from carrying spies, and others who had good reason to fear the authorities and whose movements therefore must be secret, there was one specialised form of smuggling which paid really huge dividends. It was loosely called 'guinea smuggling' and was no less than the illegal export of gold specie from ports on the South Coast to the Continent. Special boats were built for this traffic, called guinea boats, thirty or more feet in length and rowed by a crew of up to twenty-four men. They could average four knots in calm weather, making the Channel crossing from, say, Deal or Dover in about six hours.

At this time it was well known that the French obtained English gold to finance their military adventures, the merchant bankers who discounted their bills receiving as much as twenty per cent for the accommodation! Sums ranging from ten to twelve thousand guineas a week were ferried across to the Continent and it can be safely assumed the smugglers did not return empty handed.

The difficulty of finding evidence that a partisan court could not lightly dismiss, confronted the revenue officers at every turn. A cutter might overhaul and search a vessel that everyone on board knew to be a smuggler, only to find no contraband, the cargo having been sunk at some convenient spot from which it could later be recovered. On other occasions, when Preventive men actually intercepted a landing in progress they would be faced by the 'batsmen' armed with heavy clubs which they did not hesitate to use. More often than not the Preventive men were outnumbered, for the carriers would join in the

fight, determined at all costs to prevent the seizure of
boat and cargo. A Preventive officer, writing to his mother
complained bitterly that 'it was of little use to bring these
malefactors before the justices, as each and every one from
the sheriff down was a party to what was going on'!

Also, the interests involved in smuggling were such
that their organisation was well nigh perfect. For example,
when the building of the oared galleys was prohibited,
they were built quite openly in Calais and when someone
hit on the bright idea of licensing private adventurers to
equip vessels to work with the Revenue cutters every
smuggler working the coast joined. For this was nothing
but an extension of the ancient custom of issuing letters
of marque to privateers. What happened before happened
again! Smuggling paid higher dividends than the meagre
bonus earned by the capture of a lugger with contraband
aboard so that, under the protective cover of the role
assigned to them, the privateers reaped a rich harvest!

This is only one example of the almost hopeless task
facing the authorities in their attempts to suppress
smuggling. The shortage of government ships, combined
with local conditions was advanced as an excuse for
failure, but there were other factors as well. Popular feel-
ing, together with the violent opposition displayed by
those interested in maintaining the *status quo* were in
themselves sufficient, even without the corruption in high
places which took no heed of the nation's advantage but
only of their own.

During a debate in Parliament on the Smuggling Bill
of 1736 it was said in evidence that 'in some parts of the
maritime counties the whole population was so generally
engaged in smuggling that it is impossible to find a jury
that will upon trial do justice to an officer of the revenue
in any case whatsoever'. On one of the rare occasions
when a smuggler was shot and killed during a pitched
battle between smugglers and the Preventive patrol an

attempt was made, at the inquest, to bring the officer concerned in as guilty of murder!

Reference has been made to the banding together of the different groups into confederacies, some of which grew powerful enough to terrorise the countryside. Such a group was the Hawkhurst gang, which had large storehouses at various collecting points, where goods could be handed over to the parties sent from London to receive them. One of the leaders of the gang was Arthur Gray. The buildings near Hawkhurst known as Gray's Folly are believed to have been his headquarters.

Gangs such as this, like the Alfriston gang led by Stanton Collins, in time turned their attentions to other things like highway robbery and housebreaking. They never lost sight of their main occupation, however, and in 1744 abducted a Customs officer and three of his men who had tried to intercept a cargo being landed near Shoreham. On this occasion they stopped short of murder, contenting themselves with whipping their wretched victims almost to death before shipping them off to France.

Long immunity from serious interference led the Hawkhurst gang to extend its operations in various directions, so that people went about in fear of their lives. Rick burning, cattle maiming and worse were the penalties exacted for informing against them and though several attempts were made to curtail their activities little was accomplished.

It took the village of Goudhurst, on the border between Kent and Sussex to oppose by force the lawless inroads of the marauders, who had kept them in subjection for so long. Wearied of having their horses commandeered or their houses raided for food, clothes and money, a group of the villagers formed themselves into a 'Band of Militia' commanded by an ex-soldier named Sturt. Hearing of this the gang waylaid one of the villagers and, possibly by threats of torture extracted a full account of the plans drawn up and agreed to by Sturt and his companions. They freed the man and sent him back with an impudent message to the effect that, on a certain day, they would attack the village, murder everyone in it and burn the place to the ground.

Led by one Thomas Kingsmill the gang attacked the village on the day they had said they would, quite obviously expecting no real resistance. But Sturt had been busy and the attackers met with a spirited fusillade from houses and rooftops. George Kingsmill, brother of the gang's leader, was shot dead. Before the 'battle' ended two more of the gang were killed and a number wounded. The rest retreated, pursued by the victorious villagers, who took a number of prisoners whom they handed over to the authorities.

This was not the end of the Hawkhurst gang, however. Possibly no other outrage, and there were many, so shocked public opinion as did the murder of Daniel Chater and William Galley following a ʻraid on the Customs House at Poole. This came after the capture of a cargo of tea by a Revenue cutter commanded by Captain Johnson, who took the vessel into custody and lodged the tea in the Customs House.

This represented a very great loss to the smugglers and it was decided to recover the goods. Well over sixty members of the gang, armed and mounted, set out for Poole, having arranged for thirty of them to carry out the raid, and the remainder to take up positions along the route keeping a lookout for riding officers or any other kind of military activity.

The raid went off as planned. At midnight of October 6th 1747 the gang broke into the Customs House and removed the tea, 37 hundredweight in all, and returned through Fordingbridge, picking up their fellow criminals en route. One of those who saw them pass was a shoemaker called Chater, who recognised one of the smugglers whose name was Jack Diamond.

Diamond evidently remembered Chater, for he leaned from his saddle as he passed, shook hands and presented Chater with a bag of tea.

A few days later, following the issue of a proclamation offering a reward for any information that would lead to the conviction of the raiders, Diamond was arrested in Chichester. Chater let it be known that he had seen Diamond back from Poole and exhibited the bag of tea he had been given. Hearing of this, the Collector of Customs at Southampton got in touch with Chater and after much discussion persuaded him to go with William Galley, an Excise officer, to Major Battin, Commissioner of Customs at Chichester, in order to make a formal statement before witnesses concerning his ability to identify Diamond. Chater, no doubt, was chiefly concerned with collecting a reward, evidently regarding the risk of revenge by other members of the gang as slight.

Galley and Chater, therefore, set out on horseback on February the 14th, a Sunday. On their way they called at Havant and were advised to go by way of Stansted to Rowland's Castle, this route being likely to reduce their journey by a considerable number of miles. Missing a turn they called in at the New Inn in Leigh to refresh themselves and to enquire their way. They met three men at the inn, George and Thomas Austen and a Mr. Jenkes who rode with them as far as Rowland's Castle. Here they all got down and went into the White Hart Inn, kept by a Mrs. Elizabeth Payne. She was the mother of two strapping sons, both of whom lived in the village and were reputed to be smugglers.

The men drank together and it would seem that Chater was somewhat indiscreet, blurting out that he and Galley were on their way to Chichester with information concerning the raid on the Poole Customs House. Hearing this Mrs. Payne is reported to have taken one of the Austens aside saying she was afraid that the two strangers were up to no good. Austen apparently replied that the

Poole affair had nothing to do with the 'locals' and that there was nothing to fear. But Mrs. Payne was not satisfied. One of the two strangers wore the uniform of a riding officer and that, as far as she was concerned, was enough. She sent one of her sons, who was in the house at the time to contact William Jackson and William Carter, two local men who were deeply involved in smuggling.

While she was telling the newcomers of her suspicions her other son came in, bringing with him William Steel, Edmund Richards, Henry Sheerman and Samuel Downer, known locally as 'Little Sam'. The newcomers wasted no time. When Galley went out to see their horses being saddled, he ran into Jackson who knocked him down, swearing horribly. Galley got up and rushed back into the inn, declaring that anyone who laid hands on him did so at his peril as he was a King's officer.

What followed is partly conjecture, while statements by some of the others are contradictory. The men had been drinking quite heavily, which probably accounts for this, but it would appear that one of the Austens acted as peacemaker and that Galley and Chater stayed on drinking until overcome and went to sleep in an adjoining room.

While they were asleep Jackson and Carter rifled their pockets and found out all they wanted to know. Another two, John Race and Richard Penny came in and it is believed that William Steel proposed that the two men should be murdered and their bodies thrown into a well not very far away. It was Jackson, however, who awakened them by rowelling them on the forehead with his spurs after which they were dragged into the kitchen and whipped about the faces and heads until streaming with blood.

Having gone too far to draw back the gang lifted their luckless victims on to one of the horses and tied their hands and legs together, beating them with heavy whips. At two in the morning the grim procession reached the

Lieut. Edgar's grave in Lydd churchyard

Portsmouth road at Rake where they halted at what was then the Red Lion Inn. Here, according to the various statements made during their subsequent trial, the gang remained drinking, having knocked up the landlord. Galley, who was still alive, was thrust into an outhouse while Chater was put in the outhouse of a man named Mills who lived near by. As dawn was breaking they carried Galley to a grave which had been hastily dug and shovelled the earth over him without caring whether he was alive or dead. According to Mills, whose statement caused a sensation at the trial, Chater was kept chained in the outhouse until the Wednesday night. He was then taken to a well in Lady Holt Park, where he was thrown in, heavy stones and two massive gateposts being thrown in on top of him, so putting an end to as brutal and sordid an episode as can possibly be imagined.

Subsequently, with the discovery of Galley's body, the murderers were traced and arrested in various parts of the county. William Steel turned King's evidence and it is largely from his account that the whole story became known. At Chichester a special Assize was arranged for the trial which took place on January 18th 1749. All the accused were found guilty and sentenced to be hanged the following day. William Jackson cheated the hangman, however, for he had been in poor health for a long time and died in gaol on the night of the trial.

If the trial and conviction of the Rake murderers was intended to overawe the smugglers by impressing upon them the power of the law it failed in its object. In the same month Richard Hawkins was whipped to death at the Dog and Partridge Inn on Slindon Common. One of the murderers in this case was John Mills, a brother of the Richard Mills executed at Chichester for the murders of Galley and Chater. He was hanged and later hung in chains on a gibbet erected for the purpose on Slindon Common.

What *does* emerge from these and similar trials, however, is the fact that those involved in smuggling usually drew a line between their activities and cold blooded murder. Running a cargo with all the expertise of deep water fishermen was one thing. There was a certain zest about outwitting the authorites and if, as sometimes happened, a random shot found its mark in a skirmish with the Revenue men, well, fair enough! That was a risk both sides were prepared to take and there were no ill feelings. But murder was a very different matter and juries were notoriously 'down' on men who could only be described as criminals of the most desperate type.

The connivance of the local clergy in turning a blind eye to what was going on, or even allowing their churches to be used a a temporary hiding place is well known. Rottingdean, where Parson Hooker was vicar, saw many cargoes brought ashore under the noses of the Coast Blockade, while Seaford, Hastings, Winchelsea and Rye could tell of luggers almost queueing up to land their quota of contraband goods.

A story is told of the old church at Hove which, at the time, was united with the parish of Preston, services being conducted there on alternate Sundays. One Sunday the vicar, due to take the service in Hove found the doors locked and no bell ringing. The verger, who had evidently anticipated his arrival, tried to persuade his superior that he had made a mistake in the date and that it was a 'Preston Sunday'. But the vicar was adamant and finally discovered the truth. The church was housing a rich cargo of tea and brandy, the kegs in the chancel and the tea in the pulpit. We are told that the vicar, acknowledging defeat, relocked the church and after putting a notice on the door telling the parishioners he was ill, went home to bed.

Nearly all the skirmishes which took place between the smugglers and the Revenue men arose from incidents such as that which occurred when a Revenue cutter gave chase to a galley off Hastings. Upon being arrested the

Tenterden Church tower

smugglers tried to escape in a boat which had been towing behind. Eight reached the beach, and of these, two were seized by Preventive officers stationed there. At this a large company of smugglers assembled with the object of freeing the arrested men. Armed with clubs, sticks and stones they assaulted the officers, cut off their belts and took their weapons, leaving the victims stunned and bleeding by the water's edge. A reward of £200 was offered but, as was usually the case, without result.

With the end of the Napoleonic wars, the Government was free to turn its attention to the activities of the smugglers, described by one Member of Parliament as 'this continuing and intolerable drain upon the resources of the nation'. In 1816, an amphibious service known as the Coast Blockade was launched and covered a stretch of coastline from Stangate Creek in Kent to Portsmouth. It comprised parties of seamen with their own officers, who worked in groups from bases distributed along the shore.

With the establishment of the Blockade the situation changed dramatically. It got off to a bad start when a shot from the Revenue cutter *Grecian* killed a man called Baker of Hastings. From an official communication dated June 6th 1816 it would appear that great bitterness was created by the incident and that the smugglers of Hastings vowed both separately and collectively to murder the officers and men of the *Grecian* should they fall into their hands.

This new antagonism, sparked off by the killing of Baker, had its roots in the increasing efficiency of the Coast Blockade, and became intensified as cargoes were more and more frequently seized, with the inevitable consequence that the vessel carrying the contraband was confiscated. We can gain an insight into its extent from the case of a seaman named England who was handed over to the civil authorities for killing a Hastings smuggler called Swain while carrying out a routine search of various beached vessels. From a report by the officer in charge

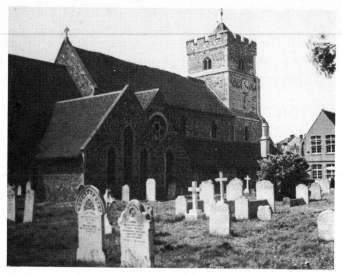

St. Leonard's, Seaford

of the Hastings Blockade we learn that the killing was accidental. The report reads:

'When England got into the fishing boat to search, the deceased resisted, striking him and throwing him out of the boat and, following him, forced the cutlass out of his hand and threw it into the sea. He then attempted to take from him his pistol. In this act he lost his life.'

A terrific fight ensued and the lieutenant and his men would have been lynched by the infuriated crowd had it not been for the timely aid rendered by the garrisons of the Martello Towers and a troop of Dragoons from Bexhill. England was tried at Horsham for murder before a packed jury and was convicted on perjured evidence, nine prosecution witnesses, all fishermen, testifying to having seen England walk behind Swain in order to shoot him through the body. No members of the Blockade had been called for the defence, nor had their depositions been returned! Despite a summing up by the judge which was heavily in favour of the accused the jury returned a verdict of

Guilty of Wilful Murder, leaving the judge with no alternative but to pass sentence of death.

However, the triumph of the Hastings smugglers was short lived. Representations by the judge, supported by detailed testimony by five of the Blockade gained England a free pardon and a discharge from further duties with the Blockade.

The Coast Blockade served a useful purpose but it suffered from the same disability as the Navy, shortage of suitable personnel. Not many naval men could be induced to volunteer and the opportunities for desertion were many. A large proportion of those who joined the Blockade deserted sooner or later and very few were recaptured. Recruits were obtained from as far afield as Ireland, which led the smugglers and their allies to complain that they were beset by foreigners!

In 1813 the Coast Blockade ceased to exist. Its place was taken by a new force, recruited from the Navy and the Revenue cutters, and given the name of 'The Preventive Water Guard'. This was later changed to the Coastguard, its duties today embracing much more than the suppression of smuggling, for it is now the guardian of all those who go down to the sea in ships.

CHAPTER VIII

Canterbury, and the Decline of the Ports

The importance of Canterbury in the history of the Confederation cannot be overemphasised. Its position as the chief cathedral town of the United Kingdom gives it a significance not shared by any other. It was the capital of Ethelbert at the time of his conversion in AD 597, when he gave his palace to St. Augustine together with the Roman church of St. Martin.

Augustine founded the Abbey which, originally a Benedictine monastery now bears his name. It was for a long time the burial place of the Kings and Queens of Kent and was held to be of greater importance than the Cathedral at that time. Augustine himself was buried there. In 758, however, Cuthbert ordered that, when he died he was to be interred in a new chapel he had caused to be built in the Cathedral. Following on this records reveal that only one other archbishop was buried in the Abbey. Becket was buried in the Cathedral after his murder and it was to the Cathedral, and not the Abbey, that Henry II made his pilgrimage to do penance for the crime. For centuries pilgrims rich and poor alike have made their way to the shrine, and the city grew prosperous on what amounted to an immense tourist traffic. Inns and lodging houses sprang up and both the Black and White Friars established communities there.

The ruins of the Abbey are impressive and show quite plainly the external length of the church. From what was the West Door to the Lady Chapel is 402 feet. Excavations have uncovered the position of earlier Saxon buildings and on the north side are the graves of the second, third and fourth archbishops. The remains were removed in 1091.

Beside the remains of the north-west tower is the great wall of the Norman nave, the top of which has been repaired with Tudor brick. It is very high and massive and the rubble cores of the Norman pillars indicate the lines of the arcades. In what was the south transept the graves of four of the Kentish kings are marked. The crypt contained three chapels, each with the remnant of its original altar. The eastern one has been restored and has a modern stone arch built over it.

Not far away and worthy of inclusion in a survey of this kind is the ruined church of St. Pancras. In the 14th century the original apse was pulled down and replaced by a squared east end, of which the great east window is still a striking feature. There are the stone foundations of

Brookland Church, *c.* 1250

what is known as St. Augustine's altar in a small chapel at the south end.

St. Martin's church, a short walk from the Abbey, is the oldest church still in use in England. Dedicated to St. Martin of Tours it was used by Queen Bertha as a Christian oratory at the time St. Augustine came to Canterbury. Ravaged and partly destroyed by the Danes, the church was repaired by the Normans and the new eastern end added. The chancel is built mainly of Roman tiles and on the north wall is a wooden carving of St. Martin dividing his cloak with the beggar. This is believed to date from about 1580.

As an example of the most blatant hypocrisy, the writ issued by Henry VIII in 1538 accusing Becket of treachery, must rank supreme. It challenged Becket's ghost to appear and to render an account of the crimes of which he was accused. The non-appearance of the Saint was seized upon as justification for the despoiling of his shrine and the confiscation of treasures from the church.

Nevertheless, despite Henry and later, the Puritans, Canterbury Cathedral remains a poem in stone where the visitor can find an atmosphere to be experienced nowhere else. In the words of Bishop Stanley: 'There is no church, no place in the kingdom . . . that is so closely connected with the history of our country as Canterbury Cathedral.' It is here that the barons of the Cinque Ports laid their silver staves and canopies after the coronation of a king and in so doing acknowledged the spiritual lordship of the Church.'

Amongst the many historical memorials to be found in the Cathedral is the tomb of the Black Prince, who died in 1376. The recumbent figure is clad in full armour, above it the replicas of the Prince's brazen gauntlets, the shield of wood and leather and the 'jupon' or coat of arms emblazoned with the arms of France and England.

At the east end is a circular chapel known as the Corona. This contains St. Augustine's chair, made of

St. George's, Ivychurch

Purbeck marble and said to date from about the beginning of the 13th century. When an archbishop is enthroned he is placed first on his thrown as Bishop of the Diocese, then in St. Augustine's Chair as Primate of All England and Metropolitan Patriarch of the English Church.

The great central tower, known as Bell Harry Tower, dominates the Cathedral both within and without. It is 235 feet high and contains Bell Harry, the great bell which is rung every evening as a curfew, and tolled on the death of a sovereign.

Before the Dissolution the Cathedral was only part of a very large and important monastic establishment. This included Lanfranc's Chapter House, rebuilt by Henry of Eastry in 1304. The library is said to be the oldest one of its kind in the English speaking world, the present building replacing the one destroyed by bombing. It contains over 30,000 books and innumerable original manuscripts, all of which are available to accredited students.

The Abbey was to have been an integral part of the

plan envisaged by St. Augustine. The Cathedral was to be the seat of the archbishops in their lifetime, while the Abbey would provide the resting place of the Kentish kings. When Augustine died in 605, however, the church was not then completed, but nevertheless, his body was interred within the walls. It is the burial place of Ethelbert and Bertha and later on, of St. Mildred, whose relics were brought here from Minster in Thanet. It thus retained its importance as a place of pilgrimage and did so up to the time of the Dissolution, when in 1538 the Abbot and his monks were forced to surrender to the King's Commissioners. The lead was stripped from the roof, the buildings partly demolished and the Abbot's lodging converted into a royal manor.

This lends support to the belief that, in 1573, Queen Elizabeth spent some time in Canterbury, where she occupied the suite of rooms where, much later, Charles I and his bride stayed in 1625. St. Augustine's was saved from final and complete destruction in 1844 by the Right. Hon. A. J. Beresford-Hope, who gave the site for the building of a college for missionaries. Damaged by bombing during the Second World War, it was closed down but in 1969 became a college for theological students.

The great West Gate, with its twin towers, stands on the site of an earlier structure. It was built by Simon of Sudbury in the 14th century and stands guardian over what was once the river crossing where most of the continental traffic converged. Strategically, it was probably one of the most important of the city's fortifications. Later, some time in the 15th century, it became the city gaol and still contains the condemned cell in what is now a very interesting museum. Not far away are the houses of the Canterbury Weavers, whose gables overhang the river. The refugee Huguenot weavers set up their looms here in 1685 and, as in the case of Sandwich, created a new and prosperous industry for the city which had given them asylum.

Some faint idea of the antiquity of Canterbury can be gleaned from the remains of an Iron Age hill fort on the road to Chartham Hatch. This is the local stronghold stormed by Caesar in 54BC. Quite close is Chaucer's 'little town' from which pilgrims obtained their first sight of the cathedral. St. Nicholas' Church here was built in 1085 as a hospital for lepers and was such for over a century.

The position of Canterbury in the hierarchy of the Ports was a delicate one. It was frequently necessary for the Archbishop to intervene in the numerous quarrels which arose between the Ports, although his authority was spiritual rather than legal. As early as the 13th century, as we have seen, the barons claimed the right of trial in Shepway and in 1248 the Sheriff of Norfolk was ordered to give mainprise to Portsmen arrested for offences at Yarmouth. The quarrels between the ports were not the only problems which beset their ecclesiastical overlords, however. It seems clear from the records that Faversham agreed to provide a ship for Dover rather than be subject to Christ Church in Canterbury. Stoner, which became a member of Sandwich in about the year 1200, chose this course, which involved submission to Sandwich. What this really meant was that members of the Confederation and their 'limbs' had not only a share in the herring fishery and freedom from toll, but also inherited, as it were, constitutional and judicial liberties which enabled them to defy their legitimate overlords, as well as to withhold their dues in money and service.

In the case of Faversham for example, the Abbot, as lord of the Manor, had rights that were jealously guarded. These included the right to appoint the beadle and the seneschal, and the aldermen had to be submitted to him for approval. Thus, when it came to a question of open defiance, culminating in the grant of a charter to Faversham, the effect of this was to give the town an

entirely new status which placed it beyond the range of
the Abbot's authority.

Association with the Cinque Ports automatically
entitled the member to the support of the Warden as well
as protection, for to infringe any of the rights conferred
by membership was to invoke the full aid of the Head
Ports. So great was the power of the Confederation at
this time that Faversham's rents and taxes were commuted
for an annual payment of £10 and it was left in possession
of the field when the Court of Shepway compelled the
archbishop to revoke an order of excommunication.

As we have seen, the progression of the Confederation
to a position of military and economic importance, with a
status almost that of an independent state was a logical
progress, if a slow one. The foundations were the need
of the King for ships, and the exceptional circumstances
which brought it into being in the first place. Long before
the welding of the Ports into a positive and integral part
of the national scene could be complete, however, the
emphasis had shifted, and by the middle of the 14th
century the Confederation had virtually ceased to exercise
any influence upon the destiny of the nation.

To begin with, although regarded as experts in naval
matters, they were no longer in a position to dictate terms
to the King. There was a growing awareness of the
country's need for a standing navy and while the Ports
continued to supply ships when called upon to do so, their
reputation for lawlessness played a part in creating
enemies who would gladly have seen their privileges
curtailed. Complaints of piracy on the high seas by
Portsmen became more and more frequent, and although
authority still turned a blind eye in the direction of such
activities, the changing situation meant that, almost overnight, the Ports had ceased to take a leading part in the
internal affairs of the country.

By the end of the 14th century their ships were no
longer required to provide the central core of the Navy as

Reculver, the twin towers

in the past, so that their services became limited to providing transport and, occasionally, reinforcements. Inevitably, a failure to recognise that they no longer belonged to a privileged minority resulted in a divergence between the local and the national interest, with the result that quarrels between the Barons and the King became more and more frequent. Fighting doggedly to uphold the privileges by which their services had once been bought, the Portsmen failed to see that the writing was on the wall. In the troubles which marked the reign of Richard II the Portsmen played no part and as neither side found it necessary to solicit their aid, they were denied the opportunity to turn the situation to their advantage.

On the available evidence it would seem, therefore, that the decline of the Ports was due almost entirely to the loss of a monopoly of naval power and very little to the geographical causes so often advanced to account for this. True, the physical changes from which the Ports suffered played their part but it is one which had been over emphasised. The changes in the coastline have continued down to the present day. What is sometimes overlooked is that the licence granted to the Ports was easily and frequently abused, and contained within it the seeds of rebellion of a kind that threatened to wreck any enterprise upon which they were engaged. Ships frequently robbed the people they had been ordered to protect and on one occasion at least, pirates at Winchelsea prevented the fleet from assembling when ordered to do so.

Numerous attempts were made to control and discipline the Portsmen and at the end of the 13th century the office of Admiral of the Cinque Ports was instituted. At first this had little or no effect, mainly because, in the beginning, those appointed were drawn chiefly from the ranks of those they were expected to control. Among those who held this office was Gervase Allard, whose tomb is in the Allard Chantry in Winchelsea church.

Another development which took place and which

136

played an important part in contributing to the curbing of the Portsmen's illicit activities was the institution of regular naval patrols. These took the place of the haphazard marauding expeditions which, more often than not, served as a cover for other and more sinister activities. This placed the Portsmen at a very considerable disadvantage, for, while it was easy enough to abandon fishing in order to give chase to some plump merchantman, the new conditions made this virtually impossible.

With the end of their monopoly, the increasing use of Royal and pressed merchant ships, the prestige and usefulness of the Cinque Ports came to an end. Some indication of the changes which took place are to be found in the records of the Hundred Years War, during which the Cinque Ports provided only a very small part of the fleets engaged in the major naval enterprises. In an exhaustive examination of the causes leading to the decline of the Ports, Miss Murray points out that during the siege of Calais in 1347, almost double the number of ships owed by the Ports under their charter were impressed from them, yet this was only one quarter of the total naval strength. In short, it was not so much that the Portsmen did less than before, but that others did more.

An important factor which must not be overlooked when reviewing the causes leading to the decline of the Confederation is that the Portsmen were first and foremost fishermen. Trading from the ports of Sandwich, Hythe and Romney in the 13th and 14th centuries was almost entirely in the hands of foreign vessels. Largely as a result the Ports were left behind in naval development so that when called upon to supply ships there was seldom any of the required tonnage available. As a result, the records give many instances of smaller members of the Confederation having to resort to chartering. It is on record that in 1514 Romney chartered four ships from Hastings.

Whether this is a contributing factor it is not possible to say with any degree of certainty, but it may well have been one of the reasons why, in the 14th century, English naval defences became inadequate against the mounting intensity of the French raids. As we have seen, the chief sufferers were the Cinque Ports and allied towns, offering as they did an attractive target easily reached. Hastings, Dover and Rye were sacked and burned. Winchelsea suffered and even Seaford, Rottingdean and Brighton were attacked. Reprisal raids directed against the French coast were launched and carried out with great ferocity but for over a century the English fleet seemed powerless to offer any real protection to the long-suffering coastline.

Faced by the need to rebuild their harbours at a time when they were crippled by the combined onslaught of war and plague, the Ports had no real chance to recover the ground they had lost. The creation, in the 15th century, of Southampton as the headquarters of the new Royal Navy sounded the death knell of the Confederation and while Dover remained the chief port for the continental traffic, the loss of other harbours was not regarded as a matter of great concern.

It is all the more remarkable, therefore, that while the Confederation had lost its chief claim to recognition there was no sign of its breaking up. There was a stringent need for economy and the development of the Brodhull, together with the extension of its power, indicates the closer association of the Ports which marked the 15th and 16th centuries. This in turn resulted in an awareness of their importance as members of a single corporation. This self esteem is well illustrated when, in 1513, it was laid down by the Brodhull that 'every man that goeth in the navy of the Ports shall have a suite of white cotyn with a red crosse and the armys of the Ports underneath, that is to say the half lyon and the half shippe'.

It would seem, therefore, that while the Queen in 1587 declared angrily that she 'doth not meane to suffer them in such fruitless manner to enjoye so great privileges without doing any service' the Ports, with the active support of the Lords Warden and backed by the ancient tradition of association, succeeded reasonably well in maintaining their position.

There was no chance of wringing further privileges from the Crown, however, for they had, quite literally, nothing to offer in exchange. The result was inevitable, for an organisation, deprived of its chief reason for existence, could only degenerate into something resembling a Merchants' Guild. The name of the Brodhull was changed to Brotherhood and this in turn became the new guardian of privilege in which an official class dominated their respective corporations and so retarded the development of popular government. The Guestling was a late and almost unnecessary addition and while the links between head port and member remained as close as ever, the only real difference between the later history of the Confederation that of a county borough is the absence of the Guild Merchant, due largely to the fact that the chief interests of the Ports lay in fishing.

Yet, despite all the factors that worked for the ending of the Confederation both in name and in fact, the spirit and traditions of the Ports will live on. One has only to stand on the sea wall at Dymchurch and look across the Marsh to understand a little of the resistant quality which is one of the most important of the characteristics of the Kent and Sussex people.

There are no others, anywhere, so deeply rooted in custom and tradition and so obstinately determined to maintain them as befits the descendants of the men who ran the gauntlet of the Revenue cutters or who sailed their ships out of the Ports to harry the lumbering Spanish galleons making their way up the Channel.

Their harbours have become silted up and in many cases have vanished. Their ports are no longer important, their sole link with the past is the fishing boats drawn up on the strand, yet they remain what they have always been, sturdily independent and with little or no use for the newcomer whose bungalows and caravan sites have so disfigured the coast. His south country dialect is as complete and perfect as it ever was, despite universal education and the proliferation of schools.

So it is with the landscape. Despite the spoliation of the coastal plain, anyone looking across the Marsh from Lympne, or from the crest of the North Downs above Folkstone sees much of what his ancestors saw when the Cinque Ports fleet sailed out of Dover to defeat the French off Sandwich. The river valleys still emphasise the roll of the Downs while the green of the turf and the white chalk pits make the same striking contrast with sea and sky that they have always done.

Even today one can capture a sense of space, of loneliness and isolation, that is to be found nowhere else in England, the treeless Downs contrasting starkly with the fertile coastal plain and the wooded Weald. Below are the coombes, which have outlasted the Roman and the Norman invasions. Modern technology has left them alone, for it would be uneconomical to attempt to develop or work their steep slopes and, small as they are, the dense woods are as primal and lonely as anything one can find. To those who know and love the countryside between the twin escarpments of the Downs, these densely wooded, steep-sided valleys stand for something that is indestructible, strongholds of isolation in which the past can be found.

To the south-east lies the Marsh with its silences, its mystery and its fascination for those with even a little imagination, while to the north can be found the valley floor of the Weald to which fragments of the once great forest of Anderida still cling. Beyond can be seen the long escarpment, holding and enclosing the land which has been so rightly called 'the cradle of England'.

October 12th 1973 was a fine, sunny day with a fresh breeze blowing in from the sea. The standard flying from the staff on the tower of St. Leonard's church in Hythe snapped and fluttered proudly in the wind as if proclaiming that an event of more than ordinary significance was about to take place.

But for the cars in the streets, it could have been October 12th in almost any year in the last seven centuries, for the town was witnessing the calling together of the Cinque Ports' Court of Brotherhood and Guestling.

Centuries have passed since the twin courts were founded, and their contribution to the nation's history is a long and colourful one. Three hundred and eighty years before, the Court of Brodhull had debated how many ships and of what tonnage the Ports could contribute to help Queen Elizabeth against the Dunkirkers. Now, for the first time in Hythe since 1910, the Court was assembling once again in the parish church to pass a resolution urging the new district council to protect the jealously guarded status of the Cinque Ports and by so doing, keep alive a tradition that had endured for nine hundred years. The medieval uniforms, the knee breeches and three cornered hats, the mace bearers with their maces carried before the mayors and aldermen of the five ports and the two 'antient towns' together with their corporate members, seemed to belong to another age. As the long procession climbed the hill to the church, led by their Speaker, the Mayor of Hythe, it was as if all that was fine and splendid in a long pageant of history had come to life. In the church, with its high roof and 13th-century chancel, the Speaker took his solitary place, facing the assembly, the silver oar of office laid crosswise before him.

In front, representatives of the Head Ports, Hythe,

Hastings, Sandwich, Dover and Romney together with Rye and Winchelsea took their places, flanked by the representatives of their corporate members, Folkestone, Lydd, Tenderden, Deal, Ramsgate, Faversham and Margate.

The proceedings were begun by a church service conducted by the Rev. Michael Kenning, of Hythe, the sermon being given by the Bishop of Dover, the Right Rev. Anthony Tremlett. He spoke briefly of the need to keep tradition alive in a world both cynical and materialistic. Only a true sense of history and its meaning, and an appreciation of the lessons it had to teach could preserve our heritage, a heritage of freedom and justice which had stood the strains and stresses of nine centuries.

The Town Sergeant of Hythe called the Court to order by the reading of a proclamation and was followed by the Senior Solicitor for the Ports, Mr. James Johnson, wearing Coronation robes and who read decrees going back to 1594. Amongst these was an ancient warning against speaking more than once on pain of being fined three shillings and fourpence!

The resolution passed, and the formal business of the Court concluded, the barons, jurats, mayors and aldermen preceded by their mace bearers filed out into the autumn sunshine, to march in slow procession back to Hythe's ancient and historic Town Hall.

It took a long time for the procession to pass and traffic waited respectfully for it to do so. When the tail vanished from sight and there was nothing more to see and wait for, it seemed as if a spell had been broken. Another page of history had been turned, perhaps for ever—who knows?

Far out to sea a passing coaster served to remind us of the proud Roman triremes making for Portus Lemanis, or the square white sails of the yellow cogs bearing the cross of St. Andrew heading out of Rye to keep watch over the narrow waters that gave the Cinque Ports birth.

Index